The Complete Gluten Free Cookbook

600 Delicious and Super Easy Recipes for Family Everyday Meals

Dr. JESSICA MCCOY

Table of Contents

INTRODUCTION

My mother, a whirlwind of boundless energy and contagious laughter, was always the queen of the kitchen. From bubbling stews to towering cakes, her creations fueled laughter and forged memories around our worn wooden table. But then, the laughter started to fade, replaced by a shadow of exhaustion and discomfort. Doctors diagnosed her with celiac disease, a gluten intolerance that turned food, once her joy, into a frustrating enemy.

Watching her navigate the aisles of the grocery store, face etched with confusion and longing, sparked a fire within me. I vowed to reclaim her joy, to rewrite the narrative where gluten wouldn't dictate her happiness. I dove headfirst into the world of gluten-free baking, a world I initially perceived as barren and bland. But what unfolded was a vibrant landscape of unexpected flavors, innovative substitutions, and a whole new kind of alchemy.

Almond flour became my canvas, coconut sugar my brushstroke, and xanthan gum my secret weapon. I whipped up almond-crusted chicken that rivaled her crispy fried masterpieces, crafted dense loaves of bread that sang with the earthiness of buckwheat, and concocted chocolate cakes that rivaled any traditional dessert. Each successful creation was a victory, a joyful shout in the face of a limiting diagnosis.

My mother's eyes, once dulled with fatigue, began to sparkle again as she savored each bite. Laughter returned, echoing through the kitchen like forgotten music. And that's when it hit me - the cookbook wasn't just about recipes, it was about reclaiming stolen joy, a testament to the boundless possibilities within the seemingly restricted world of gluten-free cooking.

This cookbook isn't just a collection of recipes; it's a love letter to my mother, a celebration of her resilience, and a beacon of hope for anyone navigating the uncharted waters of dietary restrictions. It's a testament to the transformative power of food, not just for nourishment, but for connection, laughter, and the unshakeable spirit that finds joy even in the face of limitations.

Each page whispers secrets of substitutions, shares triumphs over challenging textures, and celebrates the unexpected pairings that create magic on the plate. It's a roadmap for transforming frustration into flavor, a canvas for culinary creativity, and an invitation to join me on this delectable journey where, despite the absence of gluten, the feast is always bountiful, the laughter always abundant, and the joy in the kitchen always contagious.

So, here's to embracing the unexpected, to finding creativity in every constraint, and to proving that even when life throws you lemons (gluten-free ones, of course!), you can still make the most scrumptious lemonade. Welcome to the kitchen, because the joy of cooking, the laughter around the table, and the love shared through every bite - those are things no intolerance can ever take away.

Chapter 1: A Welcome Note

Imagine a world where fluffy biscuits crumble at the touch, the aroma of freshly baked bread is bittersweet mockery, and that decadent slice of cake is a forbidden pleasure. For many of us, this isn't just a fantastical scenario, it's the bittersweet reality of living with gluten intolerance or celiac disease. But wait, before you pack away your whisk and resign yourself to a lifetime of bland salads and dry crackers, let me whisper a secret: embracing a gluten-free journey can be an exhilarating adventure, not a culinary exile.

Witnessing the frustration and fatigue that shadowed my vibrant, food-loving mom as she grappled with celiac disease sparked a fire within me. I wouldn't let this invisible enemy steal her joy, I wouldn't let it silence the laughter that once echoed through our kitchen. So, I embarked on a mission – to rewrite the narrative, to prove that the world of gluten-free cooking wasn't one of deprivation, but one of boundless possibilities and hidden flavors.

What I discovered in the aisles of the gluten-free section wasn't a wasteland of tasteless substitutes, but a treasure trove of untapped potential. Almond flour became my canvas, coconut sugar my vibrant brushstroke, and xanthan gum my secret weapon. I conjured almond-crusted chicken that rivaled my mom's fried masterpieces, crafted dense loaves of bread that sang with the earthiness of buckwheat, and whipped up chocolate cakes so rich and decadent they sent shivers down the spines of gluten-loving skeptics. With each successful creation, the laughter returned, louder and brighter, a chorus of triumph over restriction.

And that's when it hit me: the magic wasn't just in the recipes, it was in the transformation, the reclamation of stolen joy. This cookbook isn't just a collection of gluten-free meals; it's a love letter to my mom, a celebration of her resilience, and a beacon of hope for anyone navigating the uncharted waters of dietary restrictions. It's a testament to the transformative power of food, not just for nourishment, but for connection, laughter, and the unshakeable spirit that finds joy even in the face of limitations.

Essential Tips & Tricks for Mastering Gluten-Free Cooking:

Stepping into the gluten-free kitchen might feel daunting, but fear not, culinary explorer! Here are some essential tips and tricks to unlock your inner baking guru:

Embrace the Power of Blends: Unlike its wheat counterpart, gluten-free flour isn't a one-size-fits-all deal. Embrace the magic of blends! Experiment with combinations like almond and coconut flour for delicate pastries, rice and tapioca flour for sturdy breads, and chickpea flour for savory frittatas. Remember, balance is key!

Befriend Xanthan Gum: This humble ingredient might sound intimidating, but it's your gluten-free BFF. It mimics the binding properties of gluten, preventing baked goods from crumbling into dust. Add a tiny pinch (about 1/4 teaspoon per cup of flour) for baking magic.

Hydration is Key: Gluten-free flours absorb moisture differently than wheat. Adjust your liquid levels, adding a touch more than usual initially, and remember, the texture should feel slightly sticky before baking. Trust your gut (and your finger test!).

Don't Fear Substitutions: Ran out of a specific flour? No worries! Get creative with clever substitutions. 1 cup all-purpose flour can be replaced with 1 cup of your favorite gluten-free blend + 1/2 teaspoon xanthan gum, or try swapping almond flour for a combination of oat and tapioca flour.

Patience is a Virtue: Gluten-free baking sometimes requires a little extra TLC. Don't overmix batters, let baked goods cool completely before slicing, and remember, practice makes perfect (and delicious!).

Kitchen Staples: Stocking Up for Success:

Transform your pantry into a gluten-free haven with these essential staples:

Flours: Stock up on your favorite gluten-free blend, almond flour for delicate treats, brown rice flour for versatility, and coconut flour for extra protein and density.

Starches: Tapioca starch adds moisture and softness, while potato starch helps with binding and structure. Arrowroot starch is your secret weapon for thickening sauces and soups.

Sweeteners: Coconut sugar adds a touch of caramel sweetness, while honey, maple syrup, and stevia offer variety. Remember, adjust sweetness levels based on the natural sweetness of your chosen flours.

Fats: Ghee or coconut oil are great for baking and frying, while nut butters add richness and protein. Don't forget olive oil for drizzling and avocado oil for high-heat cooking.

Nuts & Seeds: Almond flour and almond meal add richness and texture, while chia seeds and flaxseeds lend additional nutrition and fiber. Sesame seeds and chopped nuts are perfect for sprinkling on breads and topping dishes.

Baking Essentials: Xanthan gum is your binding hero, while baking powder and baking soda help your creations rise to the occasion. Vanilla extract and spices like cinnamon, nutmeg, and ginger add layers of flavor to your baking adventures.

Non-Gluten Grains: While avoiding wheat, barley, and rye, explore the wonders of gluten-free grains like quinoa, buckwheat, and millet. These versatile grains can be cooked like rice, ground into flour, or enjoyed whole in salads and bowls.

Beyond the pantry:

Invest in good quality cookware: Baking sheets, loaf pans, and muffin tins specifically designed for gluten-free baking can work wonders in preventing sticking and ensuring even baking.

Storage solutions: Store your flours and other dry ingredients in airtight containers to prevent moisture and maintain freshness. Invest in silicone baking mats for easy cleanup and a healthier alternative to parchment paper.

Embrace online resources: The internet is your gluten-free friend! Utilize dedicated websites, blogs, and social media communities for recipe inspiration, troubleshooting tips, and a supportive network of fellow gluten-free adventurers.

Embrace the experimentation, celebrate the successes (and learn from the occasional flops!), and most importantly, have fun! Cooking gluten-free doesn't have to be a chore, it can be a joyful exploration of new flavors, textures, and possibilities. This cookbook is your guide, your culinary compass, and your invitation to join me on this delicious adventure. So, preheat your oven, tie on your apron, and let's embark on a gluten-free feast for the senses!

Bonus Tip: Don't be afraid to personalize recipes! Swap spices, experiment with different fruits and vegetables, and most importantly, trust your taste buds. Your unique culinary fingerprint is what makes your gluten-free creations truly special. Let your creativity run wild and share your baking journey with the world!

Chapter 2: Breakfast & Brunch

Gluten-Free Pancakes

Serving: 4 servings

Prep Time: 10 minutes

Cooking Time: 15 minutes

Total Time: 25 minutes

Ingredients:

- 1 cup gluten-free all-purpose flour
- 2 tablespoons sugar
- 1 teaspoon baking powder
- 1/2 teaspoon baking soda
- 1/4 teaspoon salt
- 1 cup buttermilk (or dairy-free alternative)
- 1 large egg
- 2 tablespoons melted butter (or oil)
- Toppings: Berries, bananas, maple syrup

Instructions:

1. In a bowl, whisk together the gluten-free flour, sugar, baking powder, baking soda, and salt.
2. In another bowl, mix the buttermilk, egg, and melted butter.
3. Stir the dry and wet components together until they are well blended.
4. Heat a griddle or non-stick pan over medium heat and ladle the batter onto the surface.
5. Cook until surface bubbles appear, then turn and continue cooking until golden brown.
6. Serve with your favorite toppings.

Nutritional Value:

(Per serving)

- Calories: 250 kcal
- Protein: 6g
- Fat: 9g
- Carbohydrates: 38g
- Fiber: 2g

Quinoa Breakfast Bowl

Serving: 2 servings

Prep Time: 5 minutes

Cooking Time: 15 minutes

Total Time: 20 minutes

Ingredients:

- 1 cup quinoa
- 2 cups water or almond milk
- Greek yogurt
- Nuts and seeds (e.g., almonds, chia seeds)
- Honey

Instructions:

1. Rinse quinoa thoroughly and cook with water or almond milk according to package instructions.
2. Divide cooked quinoa into bowls.
3. Top with a dollop of Greek yogurt, nuts, seeds, and a drizzle of honey.

Nutritional Value:

(Per serving)

- Calories: 350 kcal
- Protein: 12g
- Fat: 8g
- Carbohydrates: 60g
- Fiber: 6g

Sweet Potato Hash with Eggs

Serving: 2 servings

Prep Time: 10 minutes

Cooking Time: 20 minutes

Total Time: 30 minutes

Ingredients:

- 2 medium sweet potatoes, diced
- 1 onion, diced
- 1 bell pepper, diced
- 4 eggs
- Salt and pepper to taste

Instructions:

1. Sauté sweet potatoes, onions, and bell peppers in a pan until tender.
2. Create wells in the hash and crack eggs into each well.
3. Cook the eggs covered until they reach your desired doneness.
4. Season with salt and pepper.

Nutritional Value:

(Per serving)

- Calories: 300 kcal
- Protein: 12g
- Fat: 10g
- Carbohydrates: 45g
- Fiber: 7g

Chia Seed Pudding

Serving: 2 servings

Prep Time: 5 minutes

Total Time: 8 hours (overnight)

Ingredients:

- 1/2 cup chia seeds
- 2 cups almond milk
- Fruits and nuts for topping

Instructions:

1. Mix chia seeds and almond milk in a bowl.
2. Cover and refrigerate overnight.
3. Stir well before serving and top with fruits and nuts.

Nutritional Value:

(Per serving)

- Calories: 200 kcal
- Protein: 6g
- Fat: 12g
- Carbohydrates: 18g
- Fiber: 10g

Gluten-Free Banana Muffins

Serving: 12 muffins

Prep Time: 15 minutes

Cooking Time: 20 minutes

Total Time: 35 minutes

Ingredients:

- 2 cups gluten-free all-purpose flour
- 1 teaspoon baking powder
- 1/2 teaspoon baking soda
- 1/4 teaspoon salt
- 3 ripe bananas, mashed
- 1/2 cup melted coconut oil
- 1/2 cup brown sugar
- 2 large eggs
- 1 teaspoon vanilla extract
- Optional: Half cup of chopped nuts or chocolate chips

Instructions:

1. Preheat the oven to 350°F (175°C) and line a muffin tin with paper As you prepare a muffin tray, line it with paper liners and preheat the oven to 350°F/175°C.
2. Mix the baking soda, baking powder, gluten-free flour, and salt in a bowl.

3. Combine the mashed bananas, eggs, brown sugar, melted coconut oil, and vanilla extract in a separate bowl.
4. Stir the dry and wet components together until they are well blended. If using, mix with chocolate chips or almonds.
5. Spoon the batter into muffin cups and bake for 18-20 minutes or until a toothpick comes out clean.
6. Allow the muffins to cool before serving.

Nutritional Value:

(Per muffin)

- Calories: 200 kcal
- Protein: 3g
- Fat: 10g
- Carbohydrates: 25g
- Fiber: 2g

Egg and Veggie Breakfast Casserole

Serving: 6 servings

Prep Time: 15 minutes

Cooking Time: 30 minutes

Total Time: 45 minutes

Ingredients:

- 8 eggs
- 1 cup diced bell peppers
- 1 cup diced onions
- 1 cup diced tomatoes
- 1 cup shredded cheese
- Salt and pepper to taste

Instructions:

1. Preheat the oven to 375°F (190°C) and grease a baking dish.
2. In a bowl, whisk the eggs and season with salt and pepper.
3. Spread diced vegetables evenly in the baking dish and pour the whisked eggs over them.
4. Sprinkle shredded cheese on top.
5. Bake for 25-30 minutes or until the eggs are set.
6. Allow the casserole to cool slightly before serving.

Nutritional Value:

(Per serving)

- Calories: 220 kcal
- Protein: 14g
- Fat: 15g
- Carbohydrates: 8g
- Fiber: 2g

Coconut Flour Waffles

Serving: 4 waffles

Prep Time: 10 minutes

Cooking Time: 15 minutes

Total Time: 25 minutes

Ingredients:

- 1 cup coconut flour
- 1 teaspoon baking powder
- 1/4 teaspoon salt
- 4 large eggs
- 1 cup almond milk (or any milk of your choice)

- 2 tablespoons melted coconut oil

Toppings: Fresh fruit, whipped cream

Instructions:

1. As directed by the manufacturer, preheat your waffle iron.
2. In a bowl, whisk together coconut flour, baking powder, and salt.
3. In another bowl, beat the eggs, then add almond milk and melted coconut oil.
4. Stir the dry ingredients into the wet mixture until well combined.
5. Once the waffle iron is hot, pour the batter over it and cook until golden brown.
6. Serve with fresh fruit or a dollop of whipped cream.

Nutritional Value:

(Per waffle)

- Calories: 180 kcal
- Protein: 7g
- Fat: 12g
- Carbohydrates: 15g
- Fiber: 8g

Smoothie Bowl

Serving: 2 bowls

Prep Time: 10 minutes

Total Time: 10 minutes

Ingredients:

2 cups mixed berries (frozen or fresh)

1 banana

1 cup spinach leaves

1/2 cup almond milk

Toppings: Gluten-free granola, seeds, coconut flakes

Instructions:

1. Blend berries, banana, spinach, and almond milk until smooth.
2. Pour the smoothie into bowls.

3. Add seeds, coconut flakes, and gluten-free granola over top.

Nutritional Value:

(Per bowl)

- Calories: 250 kcal
- Protein: 5g
- Fat: 8g
- Carbohydrates: 45g
- Fiber: 8g

Crustless Quiche

Serving: 6 servings

Prep Time: 15 minutes

Cooking Time: 35 minutes

Total Time: 50 minutes

Ingredients:

- 6 large eggs
- 1 cup milk (dairy or non-dairy)
- 1 1/2 cups shredded cheese (cheddar, Swiss, or your choice)

- 1 cup diced vegetables (spinach, bell peppers, mushrooms, etc.)
- Salt and pepper to taste

Instructions:

1. Preheat the oven to 375°F (190°C) and grease a pie dish.
2. In a bowl, whisk together eggs and milk. Add salt and pepper to taste.
3. Spread shredded cheese and diced vegetables evenly in the pie dish.
4. Pour the egg mixture over the cheese and vegetables.
5. Bake for 30-35 minutes or until the quiche is set and golden brown.
6. Allow the quiche to cool for a few minutes before serving.

Nutritional Value:

(Per serving)

- Calories: 200 kcal
- Protein: 15g
- Fat: 12g
- Carbohydrates: 8g
- Fiber: 2g

Gluten-Free Breakfast Burrito

Serving: 2 burritos

Prep Time: 10 minutes

Cooking Time: 10 minutes

Total Time: 20 minutes

Ingredients:

- 4 large eggs, scrambled
- 1 cup black beans, cooked
- 1/2 cup salsa
- 1 avocado, sliced
- 2 gluten-free tortillas

Instructions:

1. Scramble the eggs in a pan until fully cooked.
2. Warm the black beans and gluten-free tortillas.

3. Assemble the burritos by placing scrambled eggs, black beans, salsa, and sliced avocado on each tortilla.
4. Fold in the sides and roll up the burritos.

Nutritional Value:

(Per burrito)

- Calories: 400 kcal
- Protein: 18g
- Fat: 20g
- Carbohydrates: 40g
- Fiber: 12g

Rice Cake Toppings

Serving: 2 rice cakes

Prep Time: 5 minutes

Total Time: 5 minutes

Ingredients:

- 2 rice cakes
- 4 tablespoons cream cheese
- 4 slices smoked salmon
- 2 teaspoons capers

Instructions:

1. Spread cream cheese evenly on each rice cake.
2. Top with smoked salmon and sprinkle capers on top.

Nutritional Value:

(Per rice cake)

- Calories: 150 kcal
- Protein: 8g
- Fat: 10g
- Carbohydrates: 8g

Baked Avocado and Egg

Serving: 2 halves

Prep Time: 5 minutes

Cooking Time: 15 minutes

Total Time: 20 minutes

Ingredients:

- 1 avocado, halved and pitted
- 2 eggs
- Salt and pepper to taste

Optional toppings: Chopped herbs, hot sauce

Instructions:

1. Preheat the oven to 425°F (220°C).
2. Scoop out a little avocado flesh to create a larger well in each half.
3. Crack an egg into each avocado half.
4. Sprinkle with salt and pepper.
5. Bake the eggs for twelve to fifteen minutes, or until they set.
6. Top with optional herbs or hot sauce before serving.

Nutritional Value:

(Per half avocado with egg)

- Calories: 250 kcal
- Protein: 8g
- Fat: 20g
- Carbohydrates: 12g
- Fiber: 7g

Almond Flour Banana Bread

Serving: 12 slices

Prep Time: 15 minutes

Cooking Time: 50-60 minutes

Total Time: 1 hour 10 minutes

Ingredients:

- 2 cups almond flour
- 1 teaspoon baking soda
- 1/4 teaspoon salt
- 3 ripe bananas, mashed
- 1/4 cup melted coconut oil or butter
- 1/4 cup honey or maple syrup
- 3 large eggs
- 1 teaspoon vanilla extract

Optional: Half cup of chopped nuts or chocolate chips

Instructions:

1. Warm up the oven to 350°F (175°C) and coat a loaf pan with oil.
2. Mix the almond flour, baking soda, and salt together in a bowl.
3. Beat eggs, honey, melted coconut oil, mashed bananas, and vanilla extract in a separate dish.
4. Stir the dry and wet ingredients together until well combined. If using chocolate chips or nuts, fold them in.
5. When a toothpick inserted into the loaf pan comes out clean, bake the batter in the pan for 50 to 60 minutes.
6. Let cool completely before slicing the banana bread.

Nutritional Value:

(Per slice)

- Calories: 200 kcal
- Protein: 6g
- Fat: 15g
- Carbohydrates: 15g
- Fiber: 3g

Smoothie Popsicles

Serving: 6 popsicles

Prep Time: 10 minutes

Freezing Time: 4 hours

Total Time: 4 hours 10 minutes

Ingredients:

- 2 cups mixed berries (e.g., strawberries, blueberries, raspberries)
- 1 banana
- 1 cup yogurt (dairy or non-dairy)
- 1/2 cup orange juice or water

Optional: Honey or maple syrup to sweeten

Instructions:

1. Blend berries, banana, yogurt, and orange juice until smooth.
2. Taste and sweeten if needed.
3. Pour the smoothie mixture into popsicle molds.
4. Put the popsicle sticks in and freeze for four hours or longer.
5. Run molds under warm water to release popsicles before serving.

Nutritional Value:

(Per popsicle)

- Calories: 80 kcal
- Protein: 2g
- Fat: 3g
- Carbohydrates: 15g
- Fiber: 3g

Gluten-Free Blueberry Muffins

Serving: 12 muffins

Prep Time: 15 minutes

Cooking Time: 20-25 minutes

Total Time: 40 minutes

Ingredients:

- 2 cups gluten-free all-purpose flour (or almond flour)
- 1 teaspoon baking powder
- 1/2 teaspoon baking soda
- 1/4 teaspoon salt
- 1/2 cup melted coconut oil or butter
- 1/2 cup honey or maple syrup
- 2 large eggs
- 1 cup yogurt (dairy or non-dairy)
- 1 teaspoon vanilla extract
- 1 1/2 cups fresh or frozen blueberries

Instructions:

1. Preheat the oven to 350°F (175°C) and line a muffin tin with paper liners.
2. In a bowl, whisk together flour, baking powder, baking soda, and salt.
3. In another bowl, mix melted coconut oil, honey, eggs, yogurt, and vanilla extract.
4. Mix the dry and wet ingredients together, stirring just until incorporated. Fold in blueberries.
5. Spoon the batter into muffin cups and bake for 20-25 minutes or until a toothpick comes out clean.
6. Allow the muffins to cool before serving.

Nutritional Value:

(Per muffin)

- Calories: 180 kcal
- Protein: 3g
- Fat: 10g
- Carbohydrates: 20g
- Fiber: 2g

Chapter 3: Lunch & Light Bites

Quinoa Salad with Grilled Chicken

Serving: 4 servings

Prep Time: 15 minutes

Cooking Time: 15 minutes (for chicken)

Total Time: 30 minutes

Ingredients:

- 1 cup quinoa, cooked
- 1 lb grilled chicken breasts, sliced
- 1 cup cherry tomatoes, halved
- 1 cucumber, diced
- 1/2 cup feta cheese, crumbled
- For the Lemon Vinaigrette:
- 1/4 cup olive oil
- 2 tablespoons lemon juice
- 1 teaspoon Dijon mustard
- Salt and pepper to taste

Instructions:

1. In a large bowl, combine cooked quinoa, grilled chicken, cherry tomatoes, cucumber, and feta cheese.
2. Combine the ingredients for the lemon vinaigrette in a separate small bowl.
3. Over the quinoa mixture, pour the vinaigrette and toss to blend.
4. You may serve the quinoa salad cold or room temperature.

Nutritional Value:

(Per serving)

- Calories: 450 kcal
- Protein: 30g
- Fat: 20g
- Carbohydrates: 35g
- Fiber: 5g

Gluten-Free Veggie Wrap

Serving: 2 wraps

Prep Time: 10 minutes

Total Time: 10 minutes

Ingredients:

- 2 gluten-free wraps
- 1/2 cup hummus
- 1 avocado, sliced
- 2 cups mixed greens
- 1/2 cup shredded carrots
- 1 bell pepper, thinly sliced

Instructions:

1. Lay out the gluten-free wraps on a flat surface.
2. Spread a generous layer of hummus onto each wrap.
3. Arrange avocado slices, mixed greens, shredded carrots, and bell pepper on the wraps.
4. Fold the sides of the wraps and roll them tightly.
5. Cut the wraps in half diagonally and serve.

Nutritional Value:

(Per wrap)

- Calories: 350 kcal
- Protein: 10g
- Fat: 15g
- Carbohydrates: 45g
- Fiber: 8g

Zucchini Noodles with Pesto

Serving: 2 servings

Prep Time: 15 minutes

Cooking Time: 5 minutes (optional, for heating noodles)

Total Time: 20 minutes

Ingredients:

- 2 large zucchinis, spiralized into noodles
- 1/2 cup gluten-free pesto sauce

Optional: Cherry tomatoes, pine nuts, grated Parmesan for garnish

Instructions:

1. Spiralize the zucchinis into noodles.
2. Toss the zucchini noodles with the gluten-free pesto sauce until well coated.
3. Optionally, heat the noodles in a pan for 3-5 minutes or until warmed.
4. Garnish with cherry tomatoes, pine nuts, and grated Parmesan if desired.
5. Serve immediately.

Nutritional Value:

(Per serving)

- Calories: 250 kcal
- Protein: 5g
- Fat: 20g
- Carbohydrates: 15g
- Fiber: 5g

Caprese Salad Skewers

Serving: 4 servings

Prep Time: 15 minutes

Total Time: 15 minutes

Ingredients:

- 1-pint cherry tomatoes
- 1 cup fresh mozzarella balls
- Fresh basil leaves
- Balsamic glaze for drizzling
- Wooden skewers

Instructions:

1. Put a cherry tomato, a ball of mozzarella, and a leaf of basil on a skewer.
2. Arrange the skewers on a serving platter.
3. Drizzle with balsamic glaze just before serving.

Nutritional Value:

(Per serving)

- Calories: 150 kcal
- Protein: 8g
- Fat: 10g
- Carbohydrates: 8g
- Fiber: 2g

Stuffed Bell Peppers

Serving: 4 servings

Prep Time: 20 minutes

Cooking Time: 30 minutes

Total Time: 50 minutes

Ingredients:

- 2 bell peppers, halved and seeds removed
- 1 cup cooked gluten-free quinoa
- 1/2 cup black beans, drained and rinsed

- 1/2 cup corn kernels
- 1/2 cup shredded cheese (cheddar or Mexican blend)
- Salt and pepper to taste

Instructions:

1. Preheat the oven to 375°F (190°C) and grease a baking dish.
2. In a bowl, mix cooked quinoa, black beans, corn, and shredded cheese.
3. Season with salt and pepper.
4. Stuff each bell pepper half with the quinoa mixture.
5. Bake the peppers for thirty minutes, or until they are soft.
6. Serve hot.

Nutritional Value:

(Per serving)

- Calories: 250 kcal
- Protein: 10g
- Fat: 8g
- Carbohydrates: 35g
- Fiber: 6g

Cauliflower Fried Rice

Serving: 4 servings

Prep Time: 15 minutes

Cooking Time: 15 minutes

Total Time: 30 minutes

Ingredients:

- 1 medium cauliflower, grated
- 1 cup mixed vegetables (peas, carrots, corn)
- 1 cup cooked protein (chicken, shrimp, or tofu)
- 2 eggs, beaten
- 2 tablespoons gluten-free soy sauce
- Green onions for garnish

Instructions:

1. In a large skillet, stir-fry grated cauliflower and mixed vegetables until tender.
2. Push the cauliflower mixture to the side and scramble the eggs in the empty space.
3. Mix in cooked protein and gluten-free soy sauce.
4. Garnish with green onions and serve hot.

Nutritional Value:

(Per serving)

- Calories: 180 kcal
- Protein: 15g
- Fat: 8g
- Carbohydrates: 20g
- Fiber: 7g

Gluten-Free Chicken Tenders

Serving: 4 servings

Prep Time: 15 minutes

Cooking Time: 20 minutes

Total Time: 35 minutes

Ingredients:

- 1 lb chicken tenders
- 1 cup gluten-free breadcrumbs
- 1/2 cup grated Parmesan cheese
- 1 teaspoon garlic powder
- 1 teaspoon paprika
- Salt and pepper to taste
- Cooking spray

Instructions:

1. Preheat the oven to 400°F (200°C) and line a baking sheet with parchment paper.
2. In a bowl, mix gluten-free breadcrumbs, Parmesan cheese, garlic powder, paprika, salt, and pepper.
3. Coat each chicken tender in the breadcrumb mixture and place on the baking sheet.
4. Lightly spray the tenders with cooking spray.
5. Bake for twenty minutes, or until cooked through and golden brown.
6. Serve with your favorite dipping sauce.

Nutritional Value:

(Per serving)

- Calories: 250 kcal
- Protein: 30g
- Fat: 10g
- Carbohydrates: 10g
- Fiber: 1g

Mango-Avocado Quinoa Bowl

Serving: 2 servings

Prep Time: 15 minutes

Cooking Time: 15 minutes (for quinoa)

Total Time: 30 minutes

Ingredients:

- 1 cup cooked quinoa
- 1 ripe mango, diced
- 1 avocado, diced
- 1/2 cup black beans, drained and rinsed
- For Lime-Cilantro Dressing:
- Juice of 1 lime
- 2 tablespoons chopped cilantro
- 2 tablespoons olive oil
- Salt and pepper to taste

Instructions:

1. In a bowl, combine cooked quinoa, diced mango, diced avocado, and black beans.
2. In a separate small bowl, whisk together lime juice, chopped cilantro, olive oil, salt, and pepper to make the dressing.
3. Pour the dressing over the combination of quinoa and give it a little swirl.
4. Serve the quinoa bowl in individual dishes.

Nutritional Value:

(Per serving)

- Calories: 400 kcal

- Protein: 8g
- Fat: 20g
- Carbohydrates: 50g
- Fiber: 10g

Lettuce Wraps with Turkey and Avocado

Serving: 2 servings

Prep Time: 10 minutes

Total Time: 10 minutes

Ingredients:

- 8 large lettuce leaves like iceberg or butter lettuce
- 1/2 lb sliced turkey
- 1 avocado, sliced
- 1 tomato, sliced
- Lime wedges for serving

Instructions:

1. Lay out the lettuce leaves on a flat surface.
2. Fill each lettuce leaf with sliced turkey, avocado, and tomato.
3. Squeeze a lime wedge over each wrap.
4. Leave the lettuce leaves rolled up and fastened with toothpicks.
5. Serve immediately.

Nutritional Value:

(Per serving)

- Calories: 300 kcal
- Protein: 20g
- Fat: 15g
- Carbohydrates: 20g
- Fiber: 8g

Egg Salad Lettuce Wraps

Serving: 2 servings

Prep Time: 15 minutes

Cooking Time: 12 minutes (for hard-boiled eggs)

Total Time: 27 minutes

Ingredients:

- 4 hard-boiled eggs, chopped
- 1/4 cup mayonnaise (gluten-free)
- 1 teaspoon Dijon mustard
- Salt and pepper to taste
- 8 large lettuce leaves

Instructions:

1. In a bowl, combine chopped hard-boiled eggs, mayonnaise, Dijon mustard, salt, and pepper.
2. Mix until well combined.
3. Spoon the egg salad onto each lettuce leaf.
4. Lettuce leaves are rolled up to make wraps.
5. Serve the egg salad wraps chilled.

Nutritional Value:

(Per serving)

- Calories: 250 kcal
- Protein: 12g
- Fat: 20g
- Carbohydrates: 5g
- Fiber: 2g

Gluten-Free Margherita Pizza

Serving: 2 servings

Prep Time: 15 minutes

Cooking Time: 15 minutes

Total Time: 30 minutes

Ingredients:

- 1 gluten-free pizza crust
- 1/2 cup tomato sauce
- 1 cup fresh mozzarella, sliced
- Fresh basil leaves
- Olive oil for drizzling

Instructions:

1. As directed on the pizza crust container, preheat the oven.
2. Spread tomato sauce over the gluten-free pizza crust.
3. Arrange sliced fresh mozzarella on top.
4. Bake the pizza until the cheese is bubbling and melted, or as directed by the crust recipe.
5. Remove from the oven and top with fresh basil leaves.
6. Drizzle with olive oil before serving.

Nutritional Value:

(Per serving)

- Calories: 400 kcal
- Protein: 15g
- Fat: 20g
- Carbohydrates: 40g
- Fiber: 4g

Stuffed Sweet Potatoes

Serving: 4 servings

Prep Time: 10 minutes

Cooking Time: 45 minutes

Total Time: 55 minutes

Ingredients:

- 4 medium sweet potatoes
- 1 cup black beans, cooked
- 1 cup corn kernels
- 1 cup diced tomatoes
- 1 avocado, diced
- Salt and pepper to taste

Instructions:

1. Preheat the oven to 400°F (200°C).
2. Wash and pierce sweet potatoes with a fork. Bake until soft, 45 minutes or so.
3. In a bowl, mix black beans, corn, diced tomatoes, and diced avocado.
4. Cut a slit in each sweet potato and fluff the insides with a fork.
5. Stuff the sweet potatoes with the black bean mixture.
6. Season with salt and pepper.
7. Serve hot.

Nutritional Value:

(Per serving)

- Calories: 300 kcal
- Protein: 8g
- Fat: 10g
- Carbohydrates: 45g
- Fiber: 10g

Quinoa and Black Bean Bowl

Serving: 2 servings

Prep Time: 15 minutes

Cooking Time: 15 minutes (for quinoa)

Total Time: 30 minutes

Ingredients:

- 1 cup cooked quinoa
- 1 cup black beans, cooked
- 1/2 cup corn kernels
- 1 avocado, diced
- Lime wedges for squeezing

Instructions:

1. In a bowl, assemble cooked quinoa, black beans, corn, and diced avocado.
2. Squeeze lime over the bowl for added freshness.
3. Toss the ingredients gently.
4. Serve in individual bowls.

Nutritional Value:

(Per serving)

- Calories: 350 kcal
- Protein: 12g
- Fat: 15g
- Carbohydrates: 45g
- Fiber: 10g

Cucumber and Smoked Salmon Roll-Ups

Serving: 4 servings

Prep Time: 15 minutes

Total Time: 15 minutes

Ingredients:

- 1 cucumber, thinly sliced lengthwise
- 4 oz smoked salmon
- 1/2 cup cream cheese
- 2 tablespoons capers

Instructions:

1. Lay out cucumber slices on a flat surface.
2. Spread cream cheese over each cucumber slice.
3. Place smoked salmon on top of the cream cheese.

4. Sprinkle capers over the smoked salmon.
5. Roll up each cucumber slice to create roll-ups.
6. Secure with toothpicks if needed.
7. Serve chilled.

Nutritional Value:

(Per serving)

- Calories: 150 kcal
- Protein: 10g
- Fat: 10g
- Carbohydrates: 5g
- Fiber: 1g

Tomato Basil Soup with Gluten-Free Grilled Cheese

Serving: 4 servings

Prep Time: 10 minutes

Cooking Time: 25 minutes

Total Time: 35 minutes

Ingredients:

- 2 cans (28 oz) crushed tomatoes
- 1 cup vegetable broth
- 1/4 cup fresh basil, chopped
- 1 teaspoon dried oregano
- Salt and pepper to taste
- For Gluten-Free Grilled Cheese:
- 8 slices gluten-free bread
- 1 cup shredded cheddar cheese
- Butter for spreading

Instructions:

For Tomato Basil Soup:

1. In a pot, combine crushed tomatoes, vegetable broth, fresh basil, oregano, salt, and pepper.
2. Simmer for 25 minutes.
3. Puree the soup with an immersion blender until it's smooth.

4. Adjust seasoning if needed.

For Gluten-Free Grilled Cheese:

1. Toast each piece of gluten-free bread on one side.
2. Place a handful of shredded cheddar cheese between two slices, butter side facing out.
3. Cook on the grill until the bread is golden brown and the cheese has melted.
4. Slice and serve with tomato basil soup.

Nutritional Value:

(Per serving)

- Calories: 400 kcal (soup), 250 kcal (grilled cheese)
- Protein: 8g (soup), 10g (grilled cheese)
- Fat: 15g (soup), 15g (grilled cheese)
- Carbohydrates: 60g (soup), 40g (grilled cheese)
- Fiber: 10g (soup), 2g (grilled cheese)

Chapter 4: Dinners & Main Courses

Grilled Lemon Herb Chicken

Serving: 4 servings

Prep Time: 10 minutes

Marinating Time: 30 minutes

Grilling Time: 15 minutes

Total Time: 55 minutes

Ingredients:

- 4 boneless, skinless chicken breasts
- 1/4 cup lemon juice
- 1/4 cup olive oil
- 3 cloves garlic, minced
- 1 teaspoon dried oregano
- 1 teaspoon dried thyme
- Salt and pepper to taste

Instructions:

1. In a bowl, mix lemon juice, olive oil, minced garlic, dried oregano, dried thyme, salt, and pepper to create the marinade.

2. Place chicken breasts in a resealable plastic bag and pour the marinade over them. After sealing the bag, chill it for a minimum of half an hour.
3. Preheat the grill to medium-high heat.
4. Grill the chicken breasts for about 6-8 minutes per side or until fully cooked.
5. Before serving, let the chicken rest for a little while.

Nutritional Value:

(Per serving)

- Calories: 300 kcal
- Protein: 30g
- Fat: 15g
- Carbohydrates: 5g
- Fiber: 1g

Quinoa Stuffed Peppers

Serving: 4 servings

Prep Time: 20 minutes

Cooking Time: 30 minutes

Total Time: 50 minutes

Ingredients:

- 4 bell peppers, halved and seeds removed
- 2 cups cooked quinoa
- 1 cup black beans, drained and rinsed
- 1 cup corn kernels
- 1 cup diced tomatoes
- 1 teaspoon ground cumin
- 1 teaspoon chili powder
- Salt and pepper to taste

Instructions:

1. Preheat the oven to 375°F (190°C) and grease a baking dish.
2. In a bowl, combine cooked quinoa, black beans, corn, diced tomatoes, ground cumin, chili powder, salt, and pepper.
3. Stuff each bell pepper half with the quinoa mixture.
4. Bake the peppers for thirty minutes, or until they are soft.

5. Serve hot.

Nutritional Value:

(Per serving)

- Calories: 300 kcal
- Protein: 10g
- Fat: 5g
- Carbohydrates: 60g
- Fiber: 10g

Gluten-Free Spaghetti Bolognese

Serving: 4 servings

Prep Time: 15 minutes

Cooking Time: 30 minutes

Total Time: 45 minutes

Ingredients:

- 8 oz gluten-free spaghetti
- 1 lb ground meat (beef, turkey, or plant-based)
- 1 onion, finely chopped
- 2 cloves garlic, minced
- 1 can (14 oz) crushed tomatoes
- 1 teaspoon dried oregano
- 1 teaspoon dried basil
- Salt and pepper to taste
- Grated Parmesan cheese for serving

Instructions:

1. Cook gluten-free spaghetti according to package instructions.
2. In a skillet, cook ground meat over medium heat until browned. Drain excess fat.
3. Add minced garlic and sliced onion to the skillet. Simmer until tender.
4. Add the dried basil, dried oregano, smashed tomatoes, salt, and pepper and stir. Simmer for 15-20 minutes.
5. Serve the Bolognese sauce over cooked gluten-free spaghetti.
6. Sprinkle with grated Parmesan cheese before serving.

Nutritional Value:

(Per serving)

- Calories: 400 kcal
- Protein: 20g
- Fat: 10g
- Carbohydrates: 60g
- Fiber: 5g

Baked Salmon with Dill Sauce

Serving: 4 servings

Prep Time: 10 minutes

Baking Time: 15 minutes

Total Time: 25 minutes

Ingredients:

- 4 salmon fillets
- 2 tablespoons olive oil
- 1 teaspoon dried dill
- 1 teaspoon garlic powder
- Salt and pepper to taste
- For Dill Sauce:
- 1/2 cup plain yogurt (gluten-free)
- 1 tablespoon fresh dill, chopped
- 1 tablespoon lemon juice
- Salt and pepper to taste

Instructions:

1. Adjust the oven temperature to 400°F (200°C) and place parchment paper on a baking pan.
2. Arrange the salmon fillets onto the baking sheet that has been prepared.
3. Pour olive oil over the fish and season with salt, pepper, garlic powder, and dried dill.
4. Bake the salmon for 15 minutes, or until it is well cooked.
5. Make the dill sauce in a basin with yogurt, fresh dill, lemon juice, salt, and pepper while the salmon bakes.
6. Drizzle some dill sauce over the cooked fish before serving.

Nutritional Value:

(Per serving)

- Calories: 350 kcal
- Protein: 25g
- Fat: 20g
- Carbohydrates: 2g

Vegetarian Stir-Fry with Tofu

Serving: 4 servings

Prep Time: 15 minutes

Cooking Time: 15 minutes

Total Time: 30 minutes

Ingredients:

- One block (14 ounce) firm tofu, pressed and cubed
- 2 cups broccoli florets
- 1 red bell pepper, sliced

- 1 yellow bell pepper, sliced
- 1 carrot, julienned
- 1/4 cup gluten-free soy sauce
- 2 tablespoons sesame oil
- 2 cloves garlic, minced
- 1 teaspoon ginger, grated
- 2 green onions, sliced
- Cooked rice or rice noodles for serving

Instructions:

1. In a wok or large skillet, heat sesame oil over medium-high heat.
2. Add cubed tofu and stir-fry until golden brown. Take out of the wok and put aside.
3. In the same wok, add a bit more oil if needed and stir-fry broccoli, red bell pepper, yellow bell pepper, and julienned carrot until crisp-tender.
4. Add minced garlic and grated ginger to the vegetables and stir-fry for an additional minute.
5. Return the tofu to the wok and pour gluten-free soy sauce over the mixture. Toss to combine.
6. Serve the vegetarian stir-fry over cooked rice or rice noodles.
7. Garnish with sliced green onions.

Nutritional Value:

(Per serving)

- Calories: 300 kcal
- Protein: 15g
- Fat: 15g
- Carbohydrates: 30g
- Fiber: 8g

Cauliflower Pizza Crust Margherita

Serving: 2 servings

Prep Time: 20 minutes

Baking Time: 20 minutes

Total Time: 40 minutes

Ingredients:

For Cauliflower Pizza Crust:

- 1 small head cauliflower, grated
- 1 egg
- 1 cup shredded mozzarella cheese
- 1 teaspoon dried oregano
- Salt and pepper to taste

Toppings:

- 1/2 cup tomato sauce
- 1 cup fresh mozzarella, sliced
- Fresh basil leaves

Instructions:

For Cauliflower Pizza Crust:

1. Adjust the oven temperature to 425°F (220°C) and place parchment paper on a baking pan.
2. In a bowl, combine grated cauliflower, egg, shredded mozzarella, dried oregano, salt, and pepper.
3. Press the mixture onto the prepared baking sheet to form a crust.
4. Bake the crust for 20 minutes, or until it becomes golden brown.

For Margherita Toppings:

1. Spread tomato sauce over the cauliflower crust.
2. Arrange sliced fresh mozzarella on top.
3. Bake for a further five to seven minutes, or until the cheese melts.
4. Garnish with fresh basil leaves before serving.

Nutritional Value:

(Per serving)

- Calories: 300 kcal
- Protein: 20g

- Fat: 15g
- Carbohydrates: 20g
- Fiber: 5g

Gluten-Free Chicken Alfredo Pasta

Serving: 4 servings

Prep Time: 15 minutes

Cooking Time: 15 minutes

Total Time: 30 minutes

Ingredients:

- 8 oz gluten-free pasta
- 1 lb chicken breasts, cooked and sliced

- 1 cup grated Parmesan cheese
- 1 cup heavy cream
- 2 cloves garlic, minced
- Salt and pepper to taste
- Fresh parsley for garnish

Instructions:

- Cook gluten-free pasta according to package instructions.
- In a saucepan, heat heavy cream and minced garlic over medium heat.
- Grated Parmesan cheese should be added and smoothed up with a toss.
- Season with salt and pepper.
- Toss cooked pasta with the Alfredo sauce.
- Top with sliced cooked chicken.
- Garnish with fresh parsley before serving.

Nutritional Value:

(Per serving)

- Calories: 500 kcal
- Protein: 30g
- Fat: 25g
- Carbohydrates: 40g
- Fiber: 2g

Eggplant Parmesan

Serving: 4 servings

Prep Time: 20 minutes

Baking Time: 30 minutes

Total Time: 50 minutes

Ingredients:

- 1 large eggplant, sliced
- 1 cup gluten-free breadcrumbs
- 1 cup marinara sauce
- 1 cup shredded mozzarella cheese
- Fresh basil leaves for garnish

Instructions:

1. Preheat the oven to 375°F (190°C) and grease a baking dish.
2. Bread each eggplant slice in gluten-free breadcrumbs.
3. Arrange the breaded eggplant slices in the baking dish.
4. Spoon marinara sauce over each slice and sprinkle with shredded mozzarella.
5. Bake the cheese for 30 minutes, or until it becomes brown and bubbling.
6. Garnish with fresh basil leaves before serving.

Nutritional Value:

(Per serving)

- Calories: 250 kcal
- Protein: 10g
- Fat: 10g
- Carbohydrates: 30g
- Fiber: 5g

Shrimp and Quinoa Paella

Serving: 4 servings

Prep Time: 15 minutes

Cooking Time: 30 minutes

Total Time: 45 minutes

Ingredients:

- 1 cup quinoa, rinsed
- 1 lb shrimp, peeled and deveined
- 1 bell pepper, diced
- 1 cup cherry tomatoes, halved
- 1/2 teaspoon saffron threads
- 2 cups vegetable broth
- 2 cloves garlic, minced
- 1 teaspoon paprika
- Salt and pepper to taste
- Lemon wedges for serving

Instructions:

1. In a large skillet, sauté diced bell pepper and minced garlic until softened.
2. Add quinoa, saffron threads, paprika, salt, and pepper. Stir to combine.
3. After adding the vegetable broth, boil the mixture.
4. Arrange shrimp, cherry tomatoes, and lemon wedges over the quinoa mixture.
5. Cover and simmer for 20-25 minutes or until the quinoa is cooked and the shrimp are pink.
6. Fluff the quinoa with a fork and serve with lemon wedges.

Nutritional Value:

(Per serving)

- Calories: 350 kcal
- Protein: 25g
- Fat: 10g
- Carbohydrates: 40g
- Fiber: 5g

Gluten-Free Beef Tacos

Serving: 4 servings

Prep Time: 15 minutes

Cooking Time: 15 minutes

Total Time: 30 minutes

Ingredients:

- 1 lb ground beef
- 1 packet gluten-free taco seasoning
- Corn tortillas
- Shredded lettuce
- Diced tomatoes
- Shredded cheese

Optional toppings: salsa, sour cream, guacamole

Instructions:

1. Cook the ground beef until browned in a pan over medium heat.
2. Drain excess fat and add gluten-free taco seasoning according to package instructions.
3. Warm corn tortillas in a dry skillet or microwave.
4. Assemble tacos with seasoned ground beef, shredded lettuce, diced tomatoes, and shredded cheese.
5. Add optional toppings like salsa, sour cream, or guacamole.
6. Serve immediately.

Nutritional Value:

(Per serving)

- Calories: 400 kcal
- Protein: 20g
- Fat: 15g
- Carbohydrates: 40g
- Fiber: 5g

Baked Lemon Herb Cod

Serving: 4 servings

Prep Time: 10 minutes

Baking Time: 15 minutes

Total Time: 25 minutes

Ingredients:

- 4 cod fillets
- 2 tablespoons olive oil
- Juice of 1 lemon
- 1 teaspoon dried herbs (rosemary, thyme, or oregano)
- 2 cloves garlic, minced
- Salt and pepper to taste
- Lemon wedges for serving

Instructions:

1. Adjust the oven temperature to 400°F (200°C) and place parchment paper on a baking pan.
2. Cod fillets should be put on the ready baking pan.
3. In a small bowl, mix olive oil, lemon juice, dried herbs, minced garlic, salt, and pepper.

4. Brush the lemon herb mixture over each cod fillet.
5. Bake the salmon for 15 minutes, or until it flakes easily with a fork.
6. Serve with lemon wedges.

Nutritional Value:

(Per serving)

- Calories: 250 kcal
- Protein: 30g
- Fat: 10g
- Carbohydrates: 2g
- Fiber: 0g

Mushroom Risotto

Serving: 4 servings

Prep Time: 10 minutes

Cooking Time: 30 minutes

Total Time: 40 minutes

Ingredients:

- 1 cup Arborio rice
- 2 cups mushrooms, sliced
- 4 cups gluten-free vegetable broth
- 1/2 cup white wine
- 1/4 cup grated Parmesan cheese
- 2 tablespoons olive oil
- 1 onion, finely chopped
- 2 cloves garlic, minced
- Salt and pepper to taste
- Fresh parsley for garnish

Instructions:

1. Warm up the olive oil in a saucepan over medium heat.
2. Sauté chopped onion and minced garlic until softened.
3. Add Arborio rice and cook, stirring, until lightly toasted.
4. Pour in white wine and cook until mostly evaporated.

5. Gradually add gluten-free vegetable broth, one ladle at a time, stirring frequently until the liquid is absorbed.

6. Stir in sliced mushrooms and continue cooking until the rice is creamy and cooked to al dente.

7. Take off the stove and mix by stirring in the grated Parmesan cheese.

8. Season with salt and pepper, garnish with fresh parsley, and serve.

Nutritional Value:

(Per serving)

- Calories: 350 kcal
- Protein: 8g
- Fat: 10g
- Carbohydrates: 50g
- Fiber: 3g

Thai Basil Chicken Stir-Fry

Serving: 4 servings

Prep Time: 15 minutes

Cooking Time: 15 minutes

Total Time: 30 minutes

Ingredients:

- 1 lb chicken breast, thinly sliced
- 2 tablespoons gluten-free soy sauce
- 1 tablespoon oyster sauce (ensure gluten-free)
- 1 tablespoon fish sauce
- 1 tablespoon sugar
- 2 tablespoons vegetable oil
- 4 cloves garlic, minced
- 1 cup Thai basil leaves
- 1 red bell pepper, sliced
- 1 yellow bell pepper, sliced
- Cooked rice for serving

Instructions:

1. In a bowl, mix gluten-free soy sauce, oyster sauce, fish sauce, and sugar to create the marinade.
2. Marinate sliced chicken in the mixture for 10 minutes.
3. In a wok or pan, heat the vegetable oil over high heat.
4. Add minced garlic and marinated chicken. Cook the chicken by stirring it until it's done.
5. Add sliced bell peppers and Thai basil leaves. Stir-fry for an additional 2-3 minutes.
6. Serve the Thai basil chicken stir-fry over cooked rice.

Nutritional Value:

(Per serving)

- Calories: 300 kcal
- Protein: 25g
- Fat: 10g
- Carbohydrates: 25g
- Fiber: 3g

Gluten-Free Chicken Enchiladas

Serving: 4 servings

Prep Time: 20 minutes

Baking Time: 25 minutes

Total Time: 45 minutes

Ingredients:

- Two cups of cooked and shredded chicken
- One cup of shredded cheese (cheddar or Mexican blend)
- 1 cup sautéed vegetables (bell peppers, onions, etc.)
- 8 corn tortillas
- 2 cups gluten-free enchilada sauce
- Fresh cilantro for garnish
- Sour cream and guacamole for serving (optional)

Instructions:

1. Preheat the oven to 375°F (190°C) and grease a baking dish.
2. In a bowl, mix shredded chicken, shredded cheese, and sautéed vegetables.
3. Warm corn tortillas in a dry skillet or microwave to make them pliable.
4. Once each tortilla has been filled with the chicken mixture, roll it up. Place the rolled enchiladas in the prepared baking dish, seam side down.
5. Pour gluten-free enchilada sauce over the rolled enchiladas.
6. The cheese should be melted and bubbling after 25 minutes in the oven.
7. Garnish with fresh cilantro.
8. Serve with optional sour cream and guacamole on the side.

Nutritional Value:

(Per serving)

- Calories: 350 kcal
- Protein: 20g
- Fat: 15g
- Carbohydrates: 30g
- Fiber: 5g

Baked Zucchini Noodles with Pesto

Serving: 4 servings

Prep Time: 15 minutes

Baking Time: 20 minutes

Total Time: 35 minutes

Ingredients:

- 4 medium zucchinis, spiralized into noodles
- 1 cup homemade or store-bought gluten-free pesto
- Salt and pepper to taste
- Grated Parmesan cheese for garnish
- Fresh basil leaves for garnish

Instructions:

1. Preheat the oven to 375°F (190°C) and grease a baking dish.
2. Spiralize zucchinis into noodles using a spiralizer.
3. Toss the zucchini noodles with gluten-free pesto until well coated.
4. Season with salt and pepper to taste.
5. Transfer the zucchini noodles to the prepared baking dish.
6. Bake for 20 minutes or until the zoodles are tender.
7. Add some grated Parmesan cheese and some fresh basil leaves as garnish.
8. Serve hot.

Nutritional Value:

(Per serving)

- Calories: 200 kcal
- Protein: 5g
- Fat: 15g
- Carbohydrates: 10g
- Fiber: 3g

Chapter 5: Sides & Accompaniments

Roasted Vegetables with Fresh Herbs

Rainbow Roasted Root Vegetables with Honey & Thyme (Serves 4-6):

Prep Time: 15 minutes

Cooking Time: 40-45 minutes

Total Time: 55-60 minutes

Ingredients:

1. 2 large carrots, peeled and cut into thick wedges
2. 2 parsnips, peeled and cut into thick wedges
3. 2 beets, peeled and cut into thick wedges
4. 1 tablespoon olive oil
5. 1 tablespoon honey
6. One teaspoon fresh thyme leaf (or half teaspoon dried)
7. Pinch of salt and pepper

Instructions:

1. Preheat oven to 400°F (200°C). Use parchment paper to line a baking sheet.
2. Toss carrots, parsnips, and beets with olive oil, honey, thyme, salt, and pepper.
3. On the prepared baking sheet, equally distribute the veggies.
4. Roast for 40-45 minutes, or until tender and slightly browned, flipping halfway through.
5. Serve warm as a delicious side dish or enjoy as a colorful snack.

Nutritional Value per Serving (approximate):

- Calories: 150
- Fat: 5g
- Carbohydrates: 25g
- Protein: 2g
- Fiber: 5g

Balsamic Glazed Brussels Sprouts with Toasted Walnuts (Serves 4-6):

Prep Time: 10 minutes

Cooking Time: 20-25 minutes

Total Time: 30-35 minutes

Ingredients:

- 1 pound Brussels sprouts, trimmed and halved
- 1 tablespoon olive oil
- 1/4 cup balsamic vinegar
- 1 tablespoon brown sugar
- 1/2 teaspoon Dijon mustard
- 1/4 cup chopped walnuts, toasted
- Pinch of salt and pepper

Instructions:

1. Preheat oven to 400°F (200°C). Use parchment paper to line a baking sheet.
2. Add salt, pepper, and olive oil to Brussels sprouts and toss. Transfer to the lined baking sheet.
3. Roast for 20 to 25 minutes, or until soft and beginning to turn golden.
4. In a small saucepan, combine balsamic vinegar, brown sugar, and Dijon mustard. Simmer for approximately five minutes, or until the mixture begins to thicken somewhat.
5. Toss roasted Brussels sprouts with balsamic glaze and sprinkle with toasted walnuts.
6. Serve warm as a flavorful and textural side dish.

Nutritional Value per Serving (approximate):

- Calories: 120
- Fat: 8g
- Carbohydrates: 15g
- Protein: 2g
- Fiber: 3g

Spicy Harissa Roasted Cauliflower Florets with Yogurt (Serves 4-6):

Prep Time: 10 minutes

Cooking Time: 20-25 minutes

Total Time: 30-35 minutes

Ingredients:

- 1 head cauliflower, cut into florets
- 1 tablespoon olive oil
- 1 tablespoon harissa paste
- 1 teaspoon lemon juice
- 1/2 teaspoon coriander powder
- Pinch of salt and pepper
- Plain Greek yogurt (for serving)

Instructions:

1. Preheat oven to 400°F (200°C). Use parchment paper to line a baking sheet.
2. In a bowl, toss cauliflower florets with olive oil, harissa paste, lemon juice, coriander powder, salt, and pepper.
3. Spread cauliflower on the prepared baking sheet.
4. Roast until soft and beginning to turn golden brown, about 20 to 25 minutes.
5. Serve warm with a dollop of plain Greek yogurt for a cooling contrast to the spice.

Nutritional Value per Serving (approximate):

- Calories: 70
- Fat: 3g
- Carbohydrates: 5g
- Protein: 2g
- Fiber: 2g

Creamy Mashed Potatoes (Sans Spuds!)

Creamy Cauliflower Mash with Garlic & Chives (Serves 4-6):

Prep Time: 10 minutes

Cooking Time: 20-25 minutes

Total Time: 30-35 minutes

Ingredients:

- 1 head cauliflower, cut into florets
- 2 cloves garlic, minced
- 1/4 cup milk (dairy or plant-based)
- 1/4 cup Greek yogurt (optional)
- 1 tablespoon butter (optional)
- 1/4 cup chopped fresh chives
- Salt and pepper to taste

Instructions:

1. Heat up some salted water in a saucepan. Add cauliflower florets and cook for 5-7 minutes, or until tender. Drain and return to the pot.
2. Mash cauliflower with a potato masher or immersion blender until smooth.
3. Stir in milk, yogurt (if using), butter (if using), garlic, and chives. To taste, add salt and pepper for seasoning.
4. Serve warm as a low-carb alternative to traditional mashed potatoes, enjoy as a dip with crudités, or even stuff into baked chicken breasts.

Nutritional Value per Serving (approximate):

- Calories: 50
- Fat: 5g (with butter)
- Carbohydrates: 5g
- Protein: 2g
- Fiber: 2g

Roasted Parsnip & Butternut Squash Mash with Sage

(Serves 4-6):

Prep Time: 15 minutes

Cooking Time: 40-45 minutes

Total Time: 55-60 minutes

Ingredients:

- 1 parsnip, peeled and chopped
- 1/2 butternut squash, peeled and chopped
- 2 tablespoons olive oil
- One teaspoon fresh sage leaves (half teaspoon dried)
- Pinch of salt and pepper
- 1/4 cup milk (dairy or plant-based)
- 1 tablespoon butter (optional)

Instructions:

1. Preheat oven to 400°F (200°C). Toss parsnip and butternut squash with olive oil, sage, salt, and pepper.
2. Spread vegetables on a baking sheet and roast for 40-45 minutes, or until tender and slightly browned.
3. Transfer roasted vegetables to a bowl and mash with a potato masher or immersion blender.
4. Stir in milk and butter (if using) until smooth and creamy.
5. Serve warm as a delicious and colorful side dish alongside roasted chicken or pork.

Nutritional Value per Serving (approximate):

- Calories: 150
- Fat: 8g (with butter)
- Carbohydrates: 20g
- Protein: 2g
- Fiber: 4g

Creamy Coconut Mash with Tropical Fruit Salsa (Serves 4-6):

Prep Time: 20 minutes

Cooking Time: 20 minutes

Total Time: 40 minutes

Ingredients:

- 4 large potatoes, peeled and chopped
- 1 can (13.5 oz) coconut milk
- 1/4 cup lime juice
- 1/2 teaspoon ginger, grated
- 1/4 teaspoon salt
- 1/4 cup chopped mango
- 1/4 cup chopped pineapple
- 1/4 cup chopped red bell pepper
- 1/4 cup chopped red onion
- Fresh cilantro, chopped (for garnish)

Instructions:

1. Heat up some salted water in a saucepan. Add potatoes and cook for 20 minutes, or until tender. Drain and return to the pot.
2. Mash potatoes with a potato masher or immersion blender.
3. Stir in coconut milk, lime juice, ginger, and salt until smooth and creamy.
4. In a separate bowl, combine chopped mango, pineapple, red bell pepper, and red onion.
5. To serve, spoon mashed potatoes onto plates and top with tropical fruit salsa. Garnish with fresh cilantro.

Nutritional Value per Serving (approximate):

- Calories: 200
- Fat: 10g
- Carbohydrates: 30g
- Protein: 2g
- Fiber: 2g

Moroccan Quinoa Pilaf with Cherries & Almonds (Serves 4-6):

Serving Size: 1 cup cooked quinoa

Prep Time: 10 minutes

Cooking Time: 20 minutes

Total Time: 30 minutes

Ingredients:

- 1 cup quinoa, rinsed
- 1 1/2 cups vegetable broth
- 1/2 teaspoon each: ground cinnamon, smoked paprika, turmeric
- 1/4 teaspoon ground ginger
- 1/4 cup slivered almonds, toasted
- 1/4 cup dried cherries
- Salt and pepper to taste

Instructions:

1. Heat broth in a pot with spices. Bring to a simmer.
2. Stir in rinsed quinoa and cover. Reduce heat and simmer for 15 minutes, or until quinoa is fluffy and liquid is absorbed.
3. Remove from heat and fluff with a fork. Stir in toasted almonds and dried cherries.
4. Season with salt and pepper to taste. Serve warm as a flavorful side dish with roasted lamb or chicken.

Nutritional Value per Serving (approximate):

- Calories: 200
- Fat: 5g
- Carbohydrates: 30g
- Protein: 5g
- Fiber: 2g

Curried Indian Coconut Rice with Peas & Cashews

(Serves 4-6):

Serving Size: 1 cup cooked rice

Prep Time: 10 minutes

Cooking Time: 20 minutes

Total Time: 30 minutes

Ingredients:

- 1 cup basmati rice, rinsed
- 1 1/2 cups coconut milk
- 1 1/2 cups water
- 1 tablespoon curry powder
- 1/2 teaspoon each: ground turmeric, garam masala
- 1/4 cup frozen peas
- 1/4 cup chopped cashews
- Salt and pepper to taste

Instructions:

1. Combine rinsed rice, coconut milk, water, spices, and salt in a pot. Bring to a boil.
2. Reduce heat, cover, and simmer for 15 minutes, or until rice is cooked and liquid is absorbed.
3. Fluff with a fork and stir in frozen peas and cashews.
4. Season with pepper to taste. Serve warm alongside vegetable curry or grilled chicken.

Nutritional Value per Serving (approximate):

- Calories: 250
- Fat: 10g
- Carbohydrates: 35g
- Protein: 4g
- Fiber: 2g

Mexican Quinoa Pilaf with Black Beans & Corn (Serves 4-6):

Serving Size: 1 cup cooked quinoa

Prep Time: 10 minutes

Cooking Time: 20 minutes

Total Time: 30 minutes

Ingredients:

- 1 cup quinoa, rinsed
- 1 1/2 cups vegetable broth
- 1 tablespoon each: cumin, chili powder
- 1/2 teaspoon smoked paprika
- 1 can (15 oz) black beans, drained and rinsed
- 1/2 cup frozen corn
- 1/4 cup chopped cilantro
- Lime wedges (for serving)

Instructions:

1. Heat broth in a pot with spices. Bring to a simmer.
2. Stir in rinsed quinoa and cover. Reduce heat and simmer for 15 minutes, or until quinoa is fluffy and liquid is absorbed.
3. Remove from heat and fluff with a fork. Stir in black beans, corn, and cilantro.
4. Season with salt and pepper to taste. Serve warm with grilled fish or fajitas, topped with lime wedges.

Nutritional Value per Serving (approximate):

- Calories: 220
- Fat: 5g
- Carbohydrates: 30g
- Protein: 8g
- Fiber: 4g

Crispy Oven-Roasted Fries & Sweet Potato Wedges:

Crispy Garlic Parmesan Fries (Serves 4-6):

Serving Size: 1 serving (medium potato)

Prep Time: 10 minutes

Cooking Time: 20-25 minutes (oven) or 5-7 minutes (air fryer)

Total Time: 30-35 minutes (oven) or 15-20 minutes (air fryer)

Ingredients:

- 2 medium potatoes, cut into fries
- 1 tablespoon olive oil
- 1/2 teaspoon garlic powder
- 1/4 cup grated Parmesan cheese
- Salt and pepper to taste

Instructions:

1. Oven: Preheat to 425°F (220°C). Toss fries with olive oil, garlic powder, salt, and pepper. Arrange in a single layer on a baking sheet. Bake, rotating midway through, for 20 to 25 minutes, or until crisp and golden brown. Top with grated Parmesan cheese and serve right away.
2. Air fryer: Warm up to 200°C/400°F. Add salt, pepper, garlic powder, and olive oil to fries and toss.
3. Arrange in a single layer within the air fryer basket.
4. Fry until crispy and golden brown, about 5 to 7 minutes. Top with grated Parmesan cheese and serve right away.

Nutritional Value per Serving (approximate):

- Calories: 250
- Fat: 10g
- Carbohydrates: 35g
- Protein: 3g
- Fiber: 1g

Spicy Chipotle Sweet Potato Wedges with Cilantro Lime Ranch (Serves 4-6):

Serving Size: 1 serving (1 medium sweet potato)

Prep Time: 10 minutes

Cooking Time: 25-30 minutes (oven) or 15-20 minutes (air fryer)

Total Time: 35-40 minutes (oven) or 25-30 minutes (air fryer)

Ingredients:

- 1 medium sweet potato, cut into wedges
- 1 tablespoon olive oil
- 1 teaspoon chili powder
- 1/2 teaspoon chipotle powder
- 1/4 teaspoon smoked paprika
- Salt and pepper to taste

Cilantro Lime Ranch Dip:

- 1/2 cup Greek yogurt
- 1/4 cup chopped cilantro
- 1 tablespoon lime juice
- 1/2 teaspoon garlic powder
- Salt and pepper to taste

Instructions:

1. Preheat oven to 400°F (200°C). Toss sweet potato wedges with olive oil, spices, and salt and pepper. In a single layer, spread out on a baking sheet. Bake for 25-30 minutes, flipping halfway, until tender and slightly browned.
2. Air Fryer: Preheat to 400°F (200°C). Toss sweet potato wedges with olive oil, spices, and salt and pepper. Arrange in a single layer within the air fryer basket. Fry for 15-20 minutes, or until tender and slightly browned.
3. Dip: Combine all dip ingredients in a bowl and mix well.
4. Serve wedges with cilantro lime ranch dip for cooling and creamy contrast.

Nutritional Value per Serving (approximate):

- Calories: 200
- Fat: 5g
- Carbohydrates: 35g
- Protein: 3g | Fiber: 3g

Chapter 6: Sweet Treats & Desserts

Decadent Gluten-Free Cakes & Cupcakes:

Rich Chocolate Cake with Almond Flour Frosting (Serves 10-12 slices):

Serving Size: 1 slice

Prep Time: 15 minutes

Cooking Time: 30-35 minutes

Total Time: 45-50 minutes

Ingredients:

Cake:

- 1 1/2 cups almond flour
- 1/2 cup unsweetened cocoa powder
- 1 teaspoon baking powder
- 1/2 teaspoon salt
- 1/2 cup unsalted butter, softened
- 1 cup granulated sugar
- 2 large eggs
- 1 teaspoon vanilla extract
- 1/2 cup milk

Almond Flour Frosting:

- 1/2 cup unsalted butter, softened
- 3 cups powdered sugar
- 1/4 cup almond flour
- 1/4 cup milk
- 1 teaspoon vanilla extract

Instructions:

1. Preheat oven to 350°F (175°C). Grease and flour a 9x13 inch baking pan.
2. Cake: In a medium bowl, whisk together almond flour, cocoa powder, baking powder, and salt. Set aside.

3. In a separate bowl, cream together butter and sugar until light and fluffy. One egg at a time, beat in, and then mix in vanilla essence.
4. Add the dry ingredients to the wet ingredients in thirds, alternating with milk, and mix until just combined.
5. Fill prepared pan with batter, and bake for 30 to 35 minutes, or until toothpick inserted in middle comes out clean.
6. Frosting: While the cake cools, prepare the frosting by beating butter until light and fluffy. Add powdered sugar, almond flour, milk, and vanilla extract, and beat until smooth and creamy.
7. Once the cake is cool, spread the almond flour frosting on top and enjoy!

Nutritional Value per Serving (approximate):

- Calories: 350
- Fat: 20g
- Carbohydrates: 35g
- Protein: 5g
- Fiber: 2g

Vanilla Bean Cupcakes with Raspberry Swirl (Makes 12 cupcakes):

Serving Size: 1 cupcake

Prep Time: 15 minutes

Cooking Time: 20-25 minutes

Total Time: 35-40 minutes

Ingredients:

Cupcakes:

- 1 1/2 cups all-purpose flour
- 1 1/2 teaspoons baking powder
- 1/4 teaspoon salt
- 1/2 cup unsalted butter, softened
- 1 cup granulated sugar
- 2 large eggs
- 1 teaspoon vanilla extract
- 1/2 cup milk
- 1/2 teaspoon vanilla bean paste (optional)

Raspberry Swirl:

- 1/2 cup raspberry jam

Instructions:

1. Preheat oven to 350°F (175°C). Line a cupcake pan with liners.
2. Cupcakes: Flour, baking powder, and salt should all be combined in a medium-sized basin. Set aside.
3. In a separate bowl, cream together butter and sugar until light and fluffy. Beat in eggs one at a time, then stir in vanilla extract and vanilla bean paste (if using).
4. Add the dry ingredients to the wet ingredients in thirds, alternating with milk, and mix until just combined.
5. Spoon batter into cupcake liners, filling them about 3/4 full.
6. Raspberry Swirl: Gently dollop a teaspoon of raspberry jam on top of each cupcake batter. Swirl the jam into the batter with a toothpick or knife.
7. A toothpick inserted in the middle should come out clean after baking for 20 to 25 minutes.
8. Let cupcakes cool completely before frosting or enjoying plain.

Nutritional Value per Serving (approximate):

- Calories: 250
- Fat: 10g
- Carbohydrates: 35g
- Protein: 3g
- Fiber: 1g

Carrot Cake with Spiced Cream Cheese Icing (Serves 10-12 slices):

Serving Size: 1 slice

Prep Time: 20 minutes

Cooking Time: 30-35 minutes

Total Time: 50-55 minutes

Ingredients:

Cake:

- 1 1/2 cups gluten-free flour blend
- 1 teaspoon baking powder
- 1/2 teaspoon baking soda
- 1 teaspoon ground cinnamon
- 1/2 teaspoon ground ginger
- 1/4 teaspoon ground nutmeg
- 1/4 teaspoon salt
- 3 large eggs
- 1 cup granulated sugar
- 1/2 cup vegetable oil
- 1/2 cup applesauce
- 1 cup grated carrots
- 1/2 cup chopped walnuts (optional)

Spiced Cream Cheese Icing:

- 8 ounces cream cheese, softened
- 1/2 cup unsalted butter, softened
- 3 cups powdered sugar
- 1 teaspoon vanilla extract
- 1/4 teaspoon ground cinnamon
- 1/8 teaspoon ground nutmeg

Instructions:

1. Preheat oven to 350°F (175°C). Grease and flour a 9x13 inch baking pan.
2. Cake: In a medium bowl, whisk together gluten-free flour blend, baking powder, baking soda, spices, and salt. Set aside.
3. In a separate bowl, whisk together eggs, sugar, oil, and applesauce until well combined.

4. Stir in grated carrots and walnuts (if using), then gradually add the dry ingredients to the wet ingredients, mixing until just combined.
5. Fill prepared pan with batter; bake for 30 to 35 minutes, or until toothpick inserted in middle comes out clean.
6. **Spiced Cream Cheese Icing:** While the cake cools, prepare the icing by beating together cream cheese and butter until light and fluffy. Add powdered sugar, vanilla extract, cinnamon, and nutmeg, and beat until smooth and creamy.
7. Once the cake is cool, spread the spiced cream cheese icing on top in a thick layer.
8. Slice and enjoy this moist and flavorful carrot cake, a delightful gluten-free twist on a classic!

Nutritional Value per Serving (approximate):

- Calories: 300
- Fat: 15g
- Carbohydrates: 35g
- Protein: 5g
- Fiber: 2g

Creamy Cheesecakes & Mousse:

No-Bake Lemon Cheesecake (Serves 8-10 slices):

Serving Size: 1 slice

Prep Time: 15 minutes

Setting Time: 4 hours (minimum)

Total Time: 4 hours 15 minutes (minimum)

Ingredients:

Crust:

- 1 1/2 cups almond flour
- 1/2 cup rolled oats
- 1/4 cup melted butter
- 1/4 cup honey
- Pinch of salt

Filling:

- 8 ounces cream cheese, softened
- 1/2 cup powdered sugar
- 1/4 cup lemon juice
- 1 teaspoon vanilla extract
- 1/4 cup heavy cream, whipped

Instructions:

1. **Crust:** Combine almond flour, oats, melted butter, honey, and salt in a bowl. Press firmly into the bottom of a 9-inch springform pan. Refrigerate for 15 minutes.
2. **Filling:** Smoothly beat cream cheese and powdered sugar together. Stir in lemon juice and vanilla extract. Fold in whipped cream gently.
3. Pour filling over the chilled crust and smooth the top. Place in the refrigerator until firm, at least 4 hours.
4. Slice and enjoy this refreshing no-bake cheesecake, perfect for any summer gathering.

Nutritional Value per Serving (approximate):

- Calories: 300
- Fat: 20g
- Carbohydrates: 25g
- Protein: 5g
- Fiber: 2g

Chocolate Raspberry Mousse (Serves 4-6 small parfaits):

Serving Size: 1 small parfait

Prep Time: 10 minutes

Setting Time: 30 minutes (minimum)

Total Time: 40 minutes (minimum)

Ingredients:

- 8 ounces semisweet chocolate, melted
- 1/2 cup heavy cream, whipped
- 1/4 cup raspberry puree
- Fresh raspberries, for garnish

Instructions:

1. Once the chocolate has melted, gently mix it into the whipped cream.
2. Divide evenly between serving dishes.
3. Swirl in raspberry puree using a spoon to create a marbled effect.
4. Chill for a minimum of half an hour or until solidified.
5. Top with fresh raspberries before serving for a burst of color and texture.

Nutritional Value per Serving (approximate):

- Calories: 250
- Fat: 15g
- Carbohydrates: 20g
- Protein: 3g
- Fiber: 1g

Mango Coconut Cream Pie (Serves 8-10 slices):

Serving Size: 1 slice

Prep Time: 20 minutes

Setting Time: 2 hours (minimum)

Total Time: 2 hours 20 minutes (minimum)

Ingredients:

Crust:

- 1 1/2 cups gluten-free cookie crumbs
- 1/4 cup melted butter
- 1/4 cup honey

Filling:

- One can (14 ounce) full-fat coconut milk, chilled
- 1/2 cup powdered sugar
- 1 tablespoon lime juice
- 1 teaspoon vanilla extract
- 1 ripe mango, sliced

Instructions:

1. **Crust:** Combine cookie crumbs, melted butter, and honey in a bowl. Press firmly into the bottom of a 9-inch pie plate. Chill for 15 minutes.
2. **Filling:** Open the chilled coconut milk can and scoop out the solid cream portion (reserve the watery liquid for another use). Beat the coconut cream with powdered sugar, lime juice, and vanilla extract until smooth and fluffy.
3. Spread the coconut filling over the chilled crust. Top with fresh mango slices.
4. Place in the fridge until firm, preferably for two hours.
5. Slice and enjoy this tropical oasis of a pie, perfect for a light and refreshing dessert.

Nutritional Value per Serving (approximate):

- Calories: 250
- Fat: 15g
- Carbohydrates: 25g
- Protein: 2g
- Fiber: 2g

Fruity Crumbles & Cobblers:

Apple Crumble with Oat and Almond Topping (Serves 4-6):

Serving Size: 1 generous portion

Prep Time: 15 minutes

Cooking Time: 35-40 minutes

Total Time: 50-55 minutes

Ingredients:

Fruit:

- 4-5 apples, peeled, cored, and sliced
- 1 tablespoon lemon juice
- 1/4 cup brown sugar
- 1 teaspoon ground cinnamon
- 1/4 teaspoon ground nutmeg

Topping:

- 1 cup rolled oats
- 1/2 cup chopped almonds
- 1/4 cup brown sugar
- 1/4 cup cold unsalted butter, cubed
- Pinch of salt

Instructions:

1. Preheat oven to 375°F (190°C). Toss sliced apples with lemon juice, brown sugar, cinnamon, and nutmeg. Transfer to a baking dish.
2. Combine oats, almonds, brown sugar, butter, and salt in a bowl. Rub with your fingertips until crumble forms.
3. Sprinkle crumble topping evenly over apples. Bake for 35-40 minutes, or until apples are tender and bubbly and topping is golden brown.
4. Serve warm with vanilla ice cream for a cozy and comforting autumn treat.

Nutritional Value per Serving (approximate):

- Calories: 350
- Fat: 15g
- Carbohydrates: 45g
- Protein: 4g
- Fiber: 5g

Summer Berry Cobbler with Gluten-Free Biscuits (Serves 6-8):

Serving Size: 1 generous portion with biscuit

Prep Time: 20 minutes

Cooking Time: 25-30 minutes

Total Time: 45-50 minutes

Ingredients:

Berries:

- 4 cups mixed berries (strawberries, blueberries, raspberries, etc.)
- 1/4 cup granulated sugar
- 1 tablespoon cornstarch
- 1/4 teaspoon lemon zest

Biscuits:

- 1 1/2 cups gluten-free flour blend
- 1 tablespoon baking powder
- 1/4 teaspoon salt
- 1/4 cup cold unsalted butter, cubed
- 1/2 cup buttermilk or unsweetened almond milk

Instructions:

1. Preheat oven to 400°F (200°C). Toss berries with sugar, cornstarch, and lemon zest. Transfer to a baking dish.
2. Flour, baking powder, and salt should all be combined in a bowl. Cut in butter using a pastry cutter or your fingers until coarse crumbs form.
3. Stir in buttermilk or almond milk until a dough forms. Gently knead a few times.
4. Drop biscuit dough on top of berries, leaving space for them to rise. Brush with melted butter for golden brown tops.
5. Bake for 25-30 minutes, or until biscuits are golden brown and berries are bubbly.
6. Serve warm with whipped cream or ice cream for a delightful summer dessert.

Nutritional Value per Serving (approximate):

- Calories: 300
- Fat: 10g
- Carbohydrates: 40g
- Protein: 3g
- Fiber: 3g

Peach and Nectarine Crumble with Streusel Topping
(Serves 4-6):

Serving Size: 1 generous portion

Prep Time: 15 minutes

Cooking Time: 30-35 minutes

Total Time: 45-50 minutes

Ingredients:

Fruit:

- 2 peaches and 2 nectarines, pitted and sliced

- 1 tablespoon brown sugar
- 1/4 teaspoon ground cinnamon
- 1/4 teaspoon ground ginger

Streusel Topping:

- 1 1/2 cups all-purpose flour
- 1/2 cup rolled oats
- 1/2 cup brown sugar
- 1/2 cup cold unsalted butter, cubed
- Pinch of salt

Instructions:

1. Preheat oven to 375°F (190°C). Toss fruit with brown sugar, cinnamon, and ginger. Transfer to a baking dish.
2. Combine flour, oats, brown sugar, butter, and salt in a bowl. Rub with your fingertips until streusel forms.
3. Sprinkle streusel topping evenly over fruit.
4. Sprinkle streusel topping evenly over fruit. Bake for 30-35 minutes, or until fruit is tender and bubbly and streusel is golden brown.
5. Let cool slightly for the filling to thicken, then serve warm with a scoop of vanilla ice cream for a burst of creamy richness against the juicy stone fruit.

Nutritional Value per Serving (approximate):

- Calories: 350
- Fat: 15g
- Carbohydrates: 45g
- Protein: 3g
- Fiber: 5g

Double Chocolate Chip Cookies with Almond Flour

(Makes 12-15 cookies):

Serving Size: 1 cookie

Prep Time: 15 minutes

Cooking Time: 12-14 minutes

Total Time: 27-29 minutes

Ingredients:

Dry:

- 1 cup almond flour
- 1/4 cup cocoa powder
- 1/2 teaspoon baking powder
- 1/4 teaspoon salt

Wet:

- 1/2 cup unsalted butter, softened
- 1/2 cup brown sugar
- 1/4 cup granulated sugar
- 1 large egg
- 1 teaspoon vanilla extract

Chocolatey Goodness:

- 1 cup semisweet chocolate chips
- 1/2 cup chopped dark chocolate or walnuts (optional)

Instructions:

1. Preheat oven to 350°F (175°C). Use parchment paper to line a baking sheet.
2. Dry Mix: In a medium bowl, whisk together almond flour, cocoa powder, baking powder, and salt.
3. Wet Mix: In a separate bowl, cream together butter and sugars until light and fluffy. Beat in the egg and vanilla essence until well blended.
4. Gradually add the dry mix to the wet mix, mixing until just combined. Stir in chocolate chips and optional chopped chocolate or walnuts.
5. Drop dough by rounded tablespoons onto prepared baking sheet, leaving space for spreading.

6. Bake for 12-14 minutes, or until cookies are slightly golden brown and set around the edges.
7. Let cookies cool on the baking sheet for a few minutes before transferring to a wire rack to cool completely. Enjoy these chewy and deliciously nutty chocolate chip cookies!

Nutritional Value per Serving (approximate):

- Calories: 250
- Fat: 15g
- Carbohydrates: 25g
- Protein: 3g
- Fiber: 2g

Peanut Butter Brownies with a Salted Caramel Drizzle (Makes 9-12 brownies):

Serving Size: 1 brownie

Prep Time: 15 minutes

Cooking Time: 25-30 minutes

Total Time: 40-45 minutes

Ingredients:

Brownie Base:

- 1/2 cup unsalted butter, melted
- 1 cup granulated sugar
- 1/2 cup unsweetened cocoa powder
- 2 large eggs
- 1/2 cup peanut butter
- 1 teaspoon vanilla extract
- 1/2 cup all-purpose flour
- 1/4 teaspoon salt

Salted Caramel Drizzle:

- 1/2 cup brown sugar
- 1/4 cup heavy cream
- 2 tablespoons butter
- Pinch of salt

- Flaky sea salt, for garnish (optional)

Instructions:

1. Preheat oven to 350°F (175°C). Grease and flour an 8x8 inch baking pan.
2. Brownie Base: In a large bowl, whisk together melted butter and sugar until smooth. Stir in cocoa powder, eggs, peanut butter, and vanilla extract until well combined.
3. Add flour and salt, mixing until just combined. Do not overmix.
4. Evenly distribute the batter after pouring it into the pan.
5. A toothpick inserted into the middle should come out with moist crumbs after baking for 25 to 30 minutes.
6. Salted Caramel Drizzle: While the brownies cool, prepare the drizzle by combining brown sugar, heavy cream, butter, and salt in a small saucepan. Bring to a boil, then reduce heat and simmer for 5 minutes, or until thickened.
7. Let the caramel cool slightly until drizzle-able. Drizzle cooled brownies with caramel and sprinkle with flaky sea salt, if desired.
8. Cut into squares and enjoy these peanut butter-infused brownies with a decadent salted caramel drizzle!

Nutritional Value per Serving (approximate):

- Calories: 300
- Fat: 18g
- Carbohydrates: 30g
- Protein: 5g
- Fiber: 2g

Snickerdoodle Cookies with Coconut Flour (Makes 12-15 cookies):

Serving Size: 1 cookie

Prep Time: 15 minutes

Cooking Time: 10-12 minutes

Total Time: 25-27 minutes

Ingredients:

Dry:

- 1 cup coconut flour
- 1/4 teaspoon baking powder

- 1/4 teaspoon salt

Wet:

- 1/2 cup unsalted butter, softened
- 1/2 cup brown sugar
- 1 egg
- 1 teaspoon vanilla extract
- Cinnamon Sugar Coating:
- 1/4 cup granulated sugar
- 1 teaspoon ground cinnamon

Instructions:

1. Preheat oven to 350°F (175°C). Use parchment paper to line a baking sheet.
2. Dry Mix: In a medium bowl, whisk together coconut flour, baking powder, and salt.
3. Wet Mix: In a separate bowl, cream together butter and brown sugar until light and fluffy. Beat in the egg and vanilla essence until well blended.
4. Gradually add the dry mix to the wet mix, mixing until just combined. Don't overmix, as the dough will be slightly sticky.
5. Combine sugar and cinnamon in a small bowl. Roll cookie dough balls in the cinnamon sugar mixture, coating evenly.
6. Place coated dough balls on prepared baking sheet, leaving space for spreading.
7. Bake for 10-12 minutes, or until cookies are light golden brown around the edges and slightly soft in the center.
8. Let cookies cool on the baking sheet for a few minutes before transferring to a wire rack to cool completely. Enjoy these slightly denser and chewy snickerdoodles with a hint of coconut and a warm cinnamon sugar glaze!

Nutritional Value per Serving (approximate):

- Calories: 200
- Fat: 12g
- Carbohydrates: 20g
- Protein: 2g
- Fiber: 2g

Chocolate-Dipped Frozen Banana Pops (Makes 4-6 pops):

Serving Size: 1 pop

Prep Time: 10 minutes

Freezing Time: 2-3 hours

Total Time: 2 hours 10 minutes (minimum)

Ingredients:

- 2-3 ripe bananas, peeled and halved
- 1/2 cup dark chocolate chips
- 1 tablespoon coconut oil (optional, for thinning chocolate)
- Sprinkles, chopped nuts, or dried fruit (optional, for topping)

Instructions:

1. Insert popsicle sticks into the flat ends of the banana halves.
2. Line a baking sheet with parchment paper and arrange banana pops on it. Freeze for at least 2 hours, or until solid.
3. Chocolate chips should be melted in a microwave-safe basin or double boiler. Add coconut oil (if using) for a thinner consistency.
4. Dip frozen banana pops halfway into the melted chocolate, letting any excess drip off.
5. Add toppings, if desired, before the chocolate hardens.
6. Freeze pops again for 15-20 minutes, or until the chocolate sets.
7. Enjoy these healthy and refreshing frozen treats with a guilt-free indulgence of rich dark chocolate!

Nutritional Value per Serving (approximate):

- Calories: 150
- Fat: 8g
- Carbohydrates: 20g
- Protein: 2g
- Fiber: 3g

Mango Coconut Ice Cream (No Churn! Makes 4-6 servings):

- Serving Size: 1/2 cup ice cream
- Prep Time: 10 minutes
- Freezing Time: 4-6 hours
- Total Time: 4 hours 10 minutes (minimum)

Ingredients:

- 1 ripe mango, peeled and chopped
- One (13.5 oz) can of full-fat coconut milk, chilled
- 1/4 cup maple syrup or honey
- 1/2 teaspoon vanilla extract
- Pinch of salt (optional)

Instructions:

- Blend chopped mango, coconut milk, maple syrup/honey, vanilla extract, and salt (if using) until smooth and creamy.
- Pour mixture into an ice cream container or loaf pan. For at least four hours, or until solid, cover and freeze.
- Thaw slightly before scooping and enjoy this vibrant and tropical homemade ice cream, made without the need for an ice cream maker!

Nutritional Value per Serving (approximate):

- Calories: 250
- Fat: 18g
- Carbohydrates: 25g
- Protein: 4g
- Fiber: 2g

Peanut Butter Chia Seed Pudding with Berries (Makes 2 servings):

- Serving Size: 1 serving with berries
- Prep Time: 5 minutes
- Chilling Time: 4-6 hours
- Total Time: 4 hours 5 minutes (minimum)

Ingredients:

- 1/2 cup chia seeds
- 1 cup unsweetened almond milk (or other plant-based milk)
- 1/4 cup natural peanut butter
- 1 tablespoon maple syrup or honey
- 1/2 teaspoon vanilla extract
- Fresh berries, for topping

Instructions:

1. Whisk together chia seeds, almond milk, peanut butter, maple syrup/honey, and vanilla extract in a bowl. Cover and refrigerate for at least 4 hours, or until pudding thickens and sets.
2. Layer chia seed pudding in jars or glasses with fresh berries. Enjoy this delicious and nutritious dessert packed with protein and healthy fats!

Nutritional Value per Serving (approximate):

- Calories: 300
- Fat: 15g
- Carbohydrates: 30g
- Protein: 10g
- Fiber: 8g

Bonus Chapter

Embarking on a gluten-free journey doesn't mean sacrificing flavorful adventures in the kitchen. This special chapter unlocks the secrets to successful gluten-free baking, equips you with holiday feasting solutions, and whisks up lightning-fast weeknight dinners for your busy life.

Baking Basics: Gluten-Free Flour Blends & Substitutions

Gluten-free flours aren't one-size-fits-all substitutes. Understanding their unique properties is key to baking like a pro. Here's a breakdown of popular choices and their strengths:

- **Almond Flour:** A versatile, nutty wonder, ideal for delicate pastries and cookies. It absorbs moisture well, but lacks structure, so often paired with starches.
- **Coconut Flour:** High in fiber and protein, this flour lends density and a hint of tropical sweetness. Requires extra hydration and careful balancing with other flours.
- **Brown Rice Flour:** Light and neutral, it blends well with other flours for a variety of baked goods. However, lacks binding properties and can make baked goods dry.
- **Cassava Flour:** A grain-free option with a neutral flavour and good thickening power. Works well for breads and pancakes, but can be gummy if used alone.
- **Potato Starch:** This starch adds moisture and softness to baked goods, but lacks protein and can lead to crumbly textures if used in excess.

Remember, magic lies in blending! Experiment with combinations like almond and coconut flour for gluten-free cakes, rice and tapioca flour for bread, and chickpea flour for savory pancakes.

Substitution Savvy: Ran out of a specific flour? No worries! Here are some clever substitutions:

1 cup all-purpose flour = 1 cup gluten-free flour blend + 1/2 teaspoon xanthan gum (for binding)

1 cup almond flour = 3/4 cup oat flour + 1/4 cup tapioca flour

1 cup coconut flour = 2/3 cup brown rice flour + 1/3 cup tapioca flour

Holiday Favorites: Gluten-Free Thanksgiving & Christmas Delights

Holidays are meant for joyous feasts, and gluten-free doesn't mean missing out! Here are some festive recipe ideas:

Gluten-Free Herb-Crusted Roasted Turkey: Enjoy the star of
the show with a fragrant herb crust made from gluten-free breadcrumbs and aromatic herbs.

- Serving Size: 1 slice with herb crust
- Prep Time: 20 minutes
- Cooking Time: 2-2 1/2 hours
- Total Time: 2 hours 20 minutes (minimum)

Ingredients:

Herb Crust:

- 1 cup gluten-free breadcrumbs
- 1/4 cup chopped fresh parsley
- 1/4 cup chopped fresh sage
- 1/4 cup chopped fresh rosemary
- 1/4 cup melted butter
- Salt and pepper to taste

Turkey:

- 12-14 pound turkey
- Olive oil
- Salt and pepper to taste

Instructions:

1. Preheat oven to 425°F (220°C).
2. Combine breadcrumbs, herbs, and butter in a bowl. Season with salt and pepper.
3. After thoroughly drying the turkey, liberally season it with salt and pepper.
4. Loosely spread the herb mixture over the breast and upper thighs of the turkey.
5. Drizzle with olive oil and place in a roasting pan.
6. Roast for 2-2 1/2 hours, basting occasionally, until internal temperature reaches 165°F (74°C) in the thickest part of the thigh.
7. Let turkey rest for 20 minutes before carving. Enjoy the fragrant and flavorful star of the show!

Nutritional Value per Serving (approximate):

- Calories: 400
- Fat: 25g
- Carbohydrates: 10g
- Protein: 45g

Mashed Sweet Potatoes with Candied Pecans: Sweet potato puree whipped with coconut milk and topped with caramelized pecans adds a luxurious touch.

Serving Size: 1/2 cup with pecans

Prep Time: 10 minutes

Cooking Time: 20-25 minutes

Total Time: 30-35 minutes

Ingredients:

- 4 large sweet potatoes, peeled and cubed
- 1 (13.5 oz) can full-fat coconut milk
- 1/4 cup maple syrup
- 1/2 teaspoon vanilla extract
- Pinch of salt
- 1/2 cup pecan halves
- 1 tablespoon butter
- 1/4 cup brown sugar

Instructions:

1. Boil sweet potatoes until tender, about 20-25 minutes. Drain and mash.
2. Stir in coconut milk, maple syrup, vanilla extract, and salt until smooth and creamy.
3. Melt butter in a skillet over medium heat. Add pecans and brown sugar. Cook until pecans are caramelized and sugar dissolves, about 5 minutes.
4. Top mashed sweet potatoes with candied pecans before serving. Enjoy this luxurious and flavorful side dish!

Nutritional Value per Serving (approximate):

- Calories: 300
- Fat: 15g
- Carbohydrates: 40g
- Protein: 5g
- Fiber: 5g

Green Bean Casserole with Almond Flour Topping

(Serves 8-10):

- Serving Size: 1 generous portion with casserole and crispy topping
- Prep Time: 20 minutes
- Cooking Time: 25-30 minutes
- Total Time: 45-50 minutes

Ditch the Canned Soup and Embrace Fresh Flavors:

Say goodbye to the processed soups of yesteryear! This green bean casserole boasts a homemade creamy mushroom sauce simmered with aromatic herbs, offering a depth of flavor and freshness you won't find in a can. Plus, the crispy almond flour topping adds a delightful textural contrast that's both flavorful and gluten-free!

Ingredients:

Casserole:

- One pound of fresh green beans, trimmed and halved
- 1 tablespoon olive oil
- 1 onion, chopped
- 2 cloves garlic, minced
- 8 ounces sliced mushrooms
- 1 cup chicken broth
- 1/2 cup heavy cream (or full-fat coconut milk for dairy-free option)
- 1 tablespoon Dijon mustard
- 1/4 cup grated Parmesan cheese
- Salt and pepper to taste
- Almond Flour Topping:
- 1/2 cup almond flour
- 1/4 cup melted butter
- 1/4 cup chopped pecans
- 1/4 teaspoon dried thyme

Instructions:

1. Preheat oven to 375°F (190°C).
2. For two to three minutes, blanch green beans in hot water. After draining, put away.
3. In a pan over medium heat, warm the olive oil. Add the onion and simmer for approximately 5 minutes, or until softened. Sauté the garlic for a further minute.
4. Add the mushrooms and simmer for approximately 5 minutes, or until golden brown.

5. Add the Dijon mustard, parmesan cheese, heavy cream or coconut milk, chicken broth, salt, and pepper. Bring to a boil and cook for approximately five minutes, or until thickened.
6. Fold in green beans. Transfer to a baking dish.
7. Combine almond flour, melted butter, chopped pecans, and thyme in a bowl. Mix until crumbly and sprinkle generously over the casserole.
8. Bake for 25-30 minutes, or until the casserole is bubbly and the topping is golden brown.
9. Let cool slightly before serving. Enjoy this flavorful and healthy upgrade to a classic Thanksgiving side dish!

Nutritional Value per Serving (approximate):

- Calories: 250
- Fat: 15g
- Carbohydrates: 20g
- Protein: 10g
- Fiber: 5g

Cranberry Orange Sauce (Serves 8-10):

- Serving Size: 2 tablespoons vibrant sauce
- Prep Time: 10 minutes
- Cooking Time: 15-20 minutes
- Total Time: 25-30 minutes

A Burst of Brightness:

This vibrant cranberry orange sauce is more than just a condiment; it's a flavor explosion on your turkey platter! Fresh cranberries simmered with orange zest and juice create a tangy and sweet sauce that complements the richness of the turkey perfectly. Plus, it's easy to prepare and adds a pop of color to your Thanksgiving table.

Ingredients:

- 12 ounces fresh cranberries
- 1/2 cup orange juice
- 1/4 cup honey or maple syrup
- 1 teaspoon grated orange zest
- Pinch of ground cinnamon

Instructions:

1. In a saucepan, combine cranberries, orange juice, honey/maple syrup, orange zest, and cinnamon. Put over medium heat and bring to a simmer.
2. Cook, stirring occasionally, until cranberries have softened and burst, about 15-20 minutes.
3. Use an immersion blender or mash with a potato masher for a smoother sauce (optional).
4. Let cool slightly before serving. Enjoy this tangy and bright cranberry orange sauce alongside your roasted turkey for a taste of Thanksgiving magic!

Nutritional Value per Serving (approximate):

- Calories: 70
- Carbohydrates: 18g
- Protein: 0g
- Fiber: 1g

Apple Crumble with Pecan Streusel: Warm spiced apples topped with a buttery pecan streusel provide the perfect comforting finale (Serves 8-10):

Serving Size: 1 individual serving

Prep Time: 20 minutes

Cooking Time: 40-45 minutes

Total Time: 60-65 minutes

Ingredients:

Apples:

- 6-8 medium apples, peeled, cored, and sliced
- 1/4 cup brown sugar
- 1 tablespoon lemon juice
- 1/2 teaspoon ground cinnamon
- Pinch of nutmeg

Pecan Streusel:

- 1/2 cup cold butter, cubed
- 1/2 cup almond flour
- 1/2 cup rolled oats
- 1/4 cup brown sugar
- 1/4 cup chopped pecans
- 1/4 teaspoon ground cinnamon

Instructions:

1. Preheat oven to 375°F (190°C).
2. Toss sliced apples with brown sugar, lemon juice, cinnamon, and nutmeg.
3. Divide apples evenly between individual ramekins or a baking dish.
4. Combine cold butter, almond flour, oats, brown sugar, chopped pecans, and cinnamon in a food processor or bowl. Pulse until a crumbly mixture forms.
5. Sprinkle the streusel topping generously over the apples.
6. Bake for 40-45 minutes, or until the apples are tender and the streusel is golden brown.
7. Let cool slightly before serving. Enjoy this warm and comforting apple crumble with a scoop of vanilla ice cream for the perfect Thanksgiving finale!

Nutritional Value per Serving (approximate):

- Calories: 300
- Fat: 15g
- Carbohydrates: 40g
- Protein: 5g
- Fiber: 5g

Christmas:

Gluten-Free Gingerbread Cookies: These festive cookies with real ginger and molasses bring the aroma of Christmas cheer to your kitchen.

Serving Size: 1 cookie

Prep Time: 15 minutes

Cooking Time: 10-12 minutes

Total Time: 25-27 minutes

Ingredients:

Dry:

- 1 1/2 cups gluten-free flour blend
- 1/2 teaspoon baking soda
- 1/2 teaspoon ground ginger
- 1/4 teaspoon ground cinnamon

- 1/4 teaspoon ground cloves
- Pinch of salt

Wet:

- 1/2 cup unsalted butter, softened
- 1/2 cup brown sugar
- 1 egg
- 1/4 cup molasses
- 1 teaspoon vanilla extract
- Royal Icing (optional):
- Powdered sugar, meringue powder, water (follow royal icing recipe)

Instructions:

1. Preheat oven to 350°F (175°C). Use parchment paper to line a baking sheet.
2. Dry Mix: In a medium bowl, whisk together flour blend, baking soda, spices, and salt.
3. Wet Mix: In a separate bowl, cream together butter and sugar until light and fluffy. Beat in the egg and vanilla essence until well blended.
4. Gradually add the dry mix to the wet mix, mixing until just combined. Don't overmix.
5. Roll dough into 1/4-inch thick balls. Using cookie cutters, cut out the needed shapes.
6. Bake for 10-12 minutes, or until cookies are lightly golden brown around the edges.
7. Let cookies cool on the baking sheet for a few minutes before transferring to a wire rack to cool completely.
8. Decorate with royal icing (optional) and enjoy these festive gingerbread cookies with a warm mug of cocoa!

Nutritional Value per Serving (approximate):

- Calories: 150
- Fat: 5g
- Carbohydrates: 25g
- Protein: 1g
- Fiber: 1g

Peppermint Bark with Almond Flour Base: Layers of rich dark chocolate, creamy white chocolate, and a hint of peppermint create an elegant and festive treat.

Serving Size: 1 square

Prep Time: 20 minutes

Setting Time: 2 hours (minimum)

Total Time: 2 hours 20 minutes (minimum)

Ingredients:

Base:

- 1/2 cup almond flour
- 1/4 cup melted butter
- 1/4 cup honey
- Pinch of salt

Chocolate Layers:

- 1 cup semisweet chocolate chips
- 1 cup white chocolate chips
- 1/4 teaspoon peppermint extract (optional)

Instructions:

1. Lay parchment paper on a square baking pan to prepare it.
2. Base: Combine almond flour, melted butter, honey, and salt in a bowl. Coat the bottom of the prepared pan with pressure.
3. Semisweet Chocolate Layer: Melt semisweet chocolate chips in a double boiler or microwave, stirring until smooth. Pour over the almond flour base and spread evenly. Refrigerate for 30 minutes.
4. White Chocolate Layer: Melt white chocolate chips with peppermint extract (if using) in a double boiler or microwave, stirring until smooth. Pour over the chilled semisweet chocolate layer and spread evenly. Two hours in the refrigerator, or until set.
5. Break or cut into squares and enjoy this elegant and festive peppermint bark!

Nutritional Value per Serving (approximate):

- Calories: 200
- Fat: 10g
- Carbohydrates: 25g
- Protein: 1g
- Fiber: 1g

Gluten-Free Eggnog: Enjoy this traditional holiday beverage with a creamy almond milk base and warm spices, perfect for chilly nights.

Serving Size: One generous mug (approximately 1 cup)

Prep Time: 10 minutes

Cooking Time: 5 minutes

Total Time: 15 minutes

Ingredients:

- 2 cups unsweetened almond milk (or another preferred plant-based milk)
- 1 cup full-fat coconut milk (for richness and creaminess)
- 1/2 cup cashews, soaked for at least 2 hours (provides natural thickening and a smooth texture)
- 1/4 cup maple syrup (adjust to your desired sweetness)
- 1 teaspoon vanilla extract (adds depth and warmth)
- 1/4 teaspoon ground nutmeg (the quintessential eggnog spice)
- Pinch of ground cinnamon (complements the nutmeg beautifully)
- Pinch of ground cloves (a subtle hint of warming spice)

Instructions:

1. Gather your ingredients and soak the cashews: If you haven't already, soak your cashews in warm water for at least 2 hours, or overnight for maximum smoothness.
2. Blend to creamy perfection: Combine all ingredients in a high-powered blender and blend until smooth and silky. The soaked cashews should help create a luxuriously creamy texture.
3. Warm it up, or keep it cool: Choose your comfort level! Gently heat the eggnog in a saucepan over low heat, stirring occasionally, until warm and cozy. Alternatively, enjoy it chilled for a refreshing treat.
4. Garnish and sip: Pour your creamy eggnog into mugs and get creative! Garnish with a sprinkling of ground nutmeg, cinnamon, or even a dollop of whipped cream for an extra festive touch. Now settle in, curl up with a good book, and savor every sip of your deliciously cozy gluten-free eggnog.

Nutritional Value per Serving (approximate):

- Calories: 300
- Fat: 15g
- Carbohydrates: 25g
- Protein: 4g
- Fiber: 3g

Tips:

For a richer flavor, try using toasted cashews in the recipe. Simply spread them on a baking sheet and toast in the oven at 350°F (175°C) for 5-7 minutes, or until lightly golden brown.

Feel free to experiment with different spices! A pinch of allspice or ginger can add another layer of warmth and complexity to your eggnog.

This recipe is easily doubled or tripled if you're looking to satisfy a larger crowd or have some delicious leftovers for the next chilly night.

Rosemary Garlic Roasted Lamb with Butternut Squash: Impress your guests with a succulent lamb roast infused with rosemary and garlic, alongside roasted butternut squash and Brussels sprouts.

Serving Size: 1 lamb chop with vegetables

Prep Time: 20 minutes

Cooking Time: 1 hour 20 minutes

Total Time: 1 hour 40 minutes

Ingredients:

- 4-6 bone-in lamb chops
- 2 tablespoons olive oil
- 1 tablespoon chopped fresh rosemary
- 4 cloves garlic, minced
- Salt and pepper to taste
- 1 medium butternut squash, peeled and cubed
- 1 pound Brussels sprouts, trimmed and halved
- 1/4 cup chicken broth

Instructions:

1. Preheat oven to 400°F (200°C).
2. Pat lamb chops dry and season generously with salt and pepper.
3. In a small bowl, combine olive oil, rosemary, and garlic. Rub mixture onto lamb chops.
4. Arrange lamb chops in a single layer in a roasting pan. Toss butternut squash and Brussels sprouts around the chops.
5. Fill the pan's bottom with chicken broth.

6. Roast for 1 hour and 20 minutes, or until lamb reaches desired doneness and vegetables are tender and browned.
7. Baste vegetables with pan juices throughout cooking.
8. Rest lamb for 5 minutes before serving. Enjoy this impressive and flavorful holiday main course!

Nutritional Value per Serving (approximate):

- Calories: 500
- Fat: 30g
- Carbohydrates: 35g
- Protein: 40g
- Fiber: 5g

Spiced Pear Upside-Down Cake with Almond Flour:

This upside-down cake features caramelized pears nestled in a spiced almond flour cake batter, a stunning end to your Christmas feast.

Serving Size: 1 slice

Prep Time: 20 minutes

Cooking Time: 40-45 minutes

Total Time: 60-65 minutes

Ingredients:

- Caramelized Pears:
- 4 ripe pears, peeled and thinly sliced
- 1/4 cup butter
- 1/4 cup brown sugar
- 1/4 teaspoon ground cinnamon

Cake Batter:

- 1 1/2 cups almond flour
- 1/2 teaspoon baking powder
- 1/4 teaspoon ground ginger
- 1/4 teaspoon ground nutmeg
- Pinch of salt
- 1/2 cup unsalted butter, softened
- 1/2 cup honey
- 2 eggs

- 1 teaspoon vanilla extract

Instructions:

1. Preheat oven to 350°F (175°C). Grease a 9-inch round cake pan very lightly.
2. Melt butter in a skillet over medium heat to make caramelized pears. Stir add cinnamon and brown sugar until the sugar is dissolved. Arrange pear slices in a single layer in the pan, overlapping slightly. Cook for 5-7 minutes, or until caramelized and softened.
3. Cake Batter: In a medium bowl, whisk together almond flour, baking powder, spices, and salt.
4. In a separate bowl, cream together butter and honey until light and fluffy. One egg at a time, beat in, and then mix in vanilla essence.
5. Add the dry ingredients to the wet ingredients in two batches, mixing until just combined. Do not overmix.
6. Pour batter over caramelized pears in the prepared pan.
7. A toothpick put into the middle should come out clean after 40 to 45 minutes of baking.
8. Ten minutes should pass before turning the cake out onto a serving plate. If preferred, serve warm with ice cream or whipped cream. Enjoy this stunning and flavorful upside-down cake with a delicious spiced twist!

Nutritional Value per Serving (approximate):

- Calories: 300
- Fat: 15g
- Carbohydrates: 35g
- Protein: 3g
- Fiber: 2g

Quick & Easy Weeknight Dinners for Busy Lives

Even hectic weekdays deserve delicious meals. Here are some quick and easy gluten-free dinner ideas:

One-Pan Chicken Fajitas: Marinate chicken strips in Fajita seasoning, toss with bell peppers and onions, and bake on a single pan for a fuss-free dinner.

Serving Size: 1 portion with chicken, peppers, and onions

Prep Time: 15 minutes

Cooking Time: 20-25 minutes

Total Time: 35-40 minutes

Ingredients:

- 1 pound boneless, skinless chicken breasts, sliced
- 1 tablespoon Fajita seasoning
- 1 red bell pepper, sliced
- 1 green bell pepper, sliced
- 1 yellow bell pepper, sliced
- 1 onion, thinly sliced
- 1 tablespoon olive oil
- Lime wedges, for serving (optional)

Instructions:

1. Preheat oven to 400°F (200°C). Use parchment paper to line a baking sheet.
2. Toss chicken in olive oil and fajita spice. Place on the baking sheet in a single layer.
3. Add onions and bell peppers to the chicken.
4. Bake for 20 to 25 minutes, or until the veggies are crisp-tender and the chicken is cooked through.
5. Serve hot with lime wedges, if desired. Enjoy this fuss-free fajita fiesta!

Nutritional Value per Serving (approximate):

- Calories: 350
- Fat: 15g
- Carbohydrates: 30g
- Protein: 35g
- Fiber: 5g

Shrimp Scampi with Zucchini Noodles: Sauté shrimp in garlic and white wine, toss with zucchini noodles, and top with fresh parsley for a light and flavorful pasta alternative.

Serving Size: 1 portion with shrimp and zucchini noodles

Prep Time: 10 minutes

Cooking Time: 15-20 minutes

Total Time: 25-30 minutes

Ingredients:

- 1 pound large shrimp, peeled and deveined
- 2 cloves garlic, minced
- 1/4 cup dry white wine
- 1 tablespoon olive oil
- 1 zucchini, spiralized into noodles
- 1/4 cup chopped fresh parsley
- Salt and pepper to taste

Instructions:

1. In a big skillet over medium heat, warm up the olive oil. Add the garlic and heat for 30 seconds or until fragrant.
2. Add shrimp and cook until pink and cooked through, about 3-4 minutes per side.
3. Pour in white wine and simmer for 1 minute, until slightly reduced.
4. Add zucchini noodles and toss with shrimp and sauce until heated through.
5. Season with salt and pepper to taste. Garnish with parsley and serve this light and flavorful scampi masterpiece!

Nutritional Value per Serving (approximate):

- Calories: 300
- Fat: 5g
- Carbohydrates: 20g
- Protein: 30g
- Fiber: 5g

Black Bean Burgers with Mango Salsa: These satisfying burgers
pack protein and flavor with black beans, corn, and spices, topped with a vibrant mango salsa.

Serving Size: 1 burger with salsa

Prep Time: 15 minutes

Cooking Time: 10-12 minutes (per side)

Total Time: 25-27 minutes

Ingredients:

Burgers:

- One (fifteen-ounce) can of rinsed and drained black beans
- 1/2 cup corn kernels, fresh or frozen

- 1/4 cup chopped red onion
- 1/4 cup chopped cilantro
- 1/4 cup breadcrumbs
- 1 tablespoon olive oil
- 1 teaspoon cumin
- 1/2 teaspoon chili powder
- Salt and pepper to taste

Mango Salsa:

- 1 ripe mango, diced
- 1/4 red onion, finely diced
- 1 tablespoon chopped cilantro
- Juice of 1/2 lime
- Pinch of chili powder
- Salt and pepper to taste

Instructions:

1. **Burgers:** Combine all burger ingredients in a food processor and pulse until a cohesive mixture form. Shape into 4 patties.
2. **Mango Salsa:** Combine all salsa ingredients in a bowl and toss well.
3. In a pan over medium heat, warm the olive oil. Burgers should be cooked through after four to five minutes on each side.
4. Assemble burgers on buns with desired toppings and a generous dollop of mango salsa. Enjoy these flavorful and satisfying black bean burgers!

Nutritional Value per Serving (approximate):

- Calories: 300
- Fat: 10g
- Carbohydrates: 35g
- Protein: 20g
- Fiber: 10g

Tuna Melts with Avocado and Sprouts: Skip the bread and layer tuna salad with creamy avocado, fresh sprouts, and sliced tomato on lettuce leaves for a healthy and refreshing sandwich.

Serving Size: 1 "melt" on lettuce leaves

Prep Time: 10 minutes

Cooking Time: None

Total Time: 10 minutes

Ingredients:

- 1 (12-ounce) can tuna, drained and flaked
- 1/2 ripe avocado, mashed
- 1 tablespoon plain Greek yogurt or mayonnaise
- 1 tablespoon lemon juice
- 1/4 cup chopped red onion
- 1/4 cup fresh sprouts
- 1 tomato, sliced
- 2 large romaine lettuce leaves

Instructions:

1. In a bowl, combine flaked tuna, mashed avocado, yogurt/mayonnaise, lemon juice, and red onion. Season with salt and pepper to taste.
2. Spread tuna mixture onto romaine lettuce leaves. Top with fresh sprouts and sliced tomato.
3. Enjoy this healthy and refreshing twist on the classic tuna melt, bursting with creamy avocado, crunchy sprouts, and juicy tomato!

Nutritional Value per Serving (approximate):

- Calories: 250
- Fat: 15g
- Carbohydrates: 10g
- Protein: 25g
- Fiber: 5g

Salmon with Lemon Dill Sauce and Roasted Asparagus: Pan-seared salmon drizzled with a bright lemon dill sauce and served alongside roasted asparagus is a quick and elegant meal.

Serving Size: 1 portion with salmon, asparagus, and sauce

Prep Time: 10 minutes

Cooking Time: 12-15 minutes (salmon), 10-12 minutes (asparagus)

Total Time: 22-27 minutes

Ingredients:

- 2 salmon fillets
- 1 tablespoon olive oil
- Salt and pepper to taste
- 1/4 cup chopped fresh dill
- 2 tablespoons lemon juice
- 1 tablespoon Dijon mustard
- 1/4 cup low-fat sour cream
- 1 bunch asparagus, trimmed

Instructions:

1. Preheat oven to 400°F (200°C). Add salt, pepper, and olive oil to the asparagus. Spread on a baking sheet and roast for 10-12 minutes, or until tender-crisp.
2. Season salmon fillets with salt and pepper. In a pan over medium heat, warm the olive oil. Pan-sear salmon for 3-4 minutes per side, until cooked through.
3. In a small bowl, whisk together dill, lemon juice, Dijon mustard, and sour cream.
4. Plate salmon, asparagus, and drizzle with lemon dill sauce. Enjoy this quick and elegant meal with a burst of fresh flavors!

Nutritional Value per Serving (approximate):

- Calories: 400
- Fat: 20g
- Carbohydrates: 15g
- Protein: 35g
- Fiber: 5g

Made in United States
Troutdale, OR
01/09/2024

16830696R00062